Make It A Great Day

The Choice Is Yours

Volume 1

Jackie Simmons

Thank you for your
Support.

Katie Miller
Assistant Director
of the
Teen Suicide
Prevention Society

Make It A Great Day

The Choice Is Yours

Volume 1

Compiled by Jackie Simmons
with

Becky Scheliga, Cody Dakota Wooten, Danielle Silverman, Denise Thomas, Erin Strayer, Ilene Skeen, Iman Aghay, Jeannette Bridoux, Jessica Peterson, Joy Resor, Joyce Blue, Kate Frank, Katie Miller, Ken Streater, Kris Bell, Lil Barcaski, Linnea Appleby, Mary Schrank, Mike Jones, Nadine Vernon, Rebeca Forero, Shauna E. VanderHoek, Stephanie Ashton, Valerie I. LaBoy, Wendy Cooper

Spotlight PUBLISHING

Goodyear, AZ

For more information, contact: Teen Suicide Prevention Society
info@teensuicidepreventionsociety.com

Why this book...

I opened the front door exhausted.

The emergency room had taken hours and it broke my heart when they pulled everything out of the room and basically locked my daughter up to keep her safe from herself as they stopped the bleeding from her arm.

The house was quiet. It was supposed to be empty, the man who had been living off my daughter's goodwill was supposed to have packed up and gotten out while I had her at the hospital.

Something was wrong, I could feel it.

Slowly opening each door, I saw the blood on the floor. . . still dripping from his butchered arm, the knife still in his other hand.

He was unconscious, still breathing... 911

With the operator in my ear, we removed the knife and waited for the ambulance. My youngest daughter holding my hand as we stared at the man whose presence was so important to her sister that she cut open her arm in an attempt to keep me from evicting him.

There was something odd about his arm… it was swollen from what appeared to be 20 or 30 shallow cuts.

So different from the cut on my daughter's arm that was clean and deep.

I can still see both in my mind.

Fast forward.

Now, I understand that while every suicide attempt is self-injury, not every act of self-injury is an attempt at suicide.

Now, I see his act as a desperate attempt to get back into the system by a man about to become homeless, and I can see his pain.

Watching the police escort him to the ambulance, I saw only betrayal. He had betrayed my daughter's trust, he had betrayed my desire for a peaceful home, he had lied about leaving, but then, he had lied about a lot of things. People in pain often do. And people in pain often self-medicate with drugs and alcohol.

There's no moral to this story, there's only the question of how to help people who are in so much emotional pain that they would harm themselves and betray those who care about them.

It's an attempt to answer that question that pushed a group of us, including my daughters, to write this book.

Inside these pages you'll find our stories. Some are fun, some have dog turds, and all are full of the tips and tricks that we use to choose to make it a great day.

We hope you enjoy the journey with us and share this book with others.

It is with the utmost gratitude that I thank those who were early sponsors and founders of this program. We started with this book and grew into a movement.

We designed this book to be a companion on the road to developing emotional resilience so that everyone will forever be able to choose to make it a great day.

If you know someone who's struggling, or you are someone who's struggling, our prescription is the same – don't wait – right now reach out for a hug and then keep reaching out.

Don't quit...

We believe heaven doesn't need another angel, we believe that heaven knows, there's someone who needs you here.

Hugs,

Jackie

*To learn more about the Teen Suicide Prevention Society and to support the movement to make suicide a thing of the past, visit: www.TeenSuicidePreventionSociety.org

Have "The Talk" to Stop Teen Suicide Based on the January 16, 2021 – TEDx TenayaPaseo Talk

In the next 24 hours, over 3,000 American teens will attempt to take their own lives.

17 of them will die.

According to the Bureau of Health Statistics, teen deaths from suicide outnumber teen deaths from diabetes, heart disease, cancer, and homicide.

The Center for Disease Control states that 25% of American Young Adults are struggling with suicidal thoughts.

This is more than double what it was just 2 years ago.

Teen suicide is a growing and contagious, epidemic.

26 years ago, my daughters were in middle school and high school. We were a stable, middle-class, American

family. Life was as predictable as you can imagine with 3 teenage girls.

It was June 1995, the start of summer vacation. The girls were getting ready for their summer visit with their dad and his family, one state away. That meant shopping!

My daughter, Stephanie, was 14. She was in-between her sisters, in-between schools, and in-between clothing sizes. The shopping was an adventure. Outfit after outfit, store after store, nothing fit her. At the end of the day, we came home with nothing... except an attitude.

Stephanie headed straight upstairs to the bathroom, and I collapsed on the sofa, grateful to be off my feet. Peace and quiet . . .

Then, "Mom, I think I need help . . ."

My eyes were drawn to Stephanie's left arm. Blood was dripping down her fingers onto the wood floor.

The emotional part of my brain started screaming in terror at the sight of my bleeding, obviously suicidal, child. The rational part of my brain started flipping through the files in my head, looking for the date of her last tetanus shot.

I wrapped her in my arms and assessed the wounds. They were not life threatening.

Have you ever felt panicky and calm at the same time?

We applied bandages and made plans to visit the teen mental health facility the next day.

Our tears finally stopped. Our mutual "I'm sorrys" were shared.

Stephanie slept.

I couldn't risk being away from her, so we were sleeping in the living room. Between us was a hand-written note. Her promise not to harm herself again while I slept.

Yeah, right, like I was going to close my eyes that night.

All night, I stared into the darkness and listened to her breathe, grateful she was still alive.

My thoughts whirled between: "what just happened?" – "how did this happen?" to: "who's to blame?" It had to be somebody's fault, right???

What followed . . . years of counseling, therapy, medications, hospitalizations, interventions, and 13, yes – 13 more attempts.

Stephanie getting professional help made it easy for me to sell myself on the idea that we didn't need to talk about it.

I didn't want to talk about it. Would you?

Would you want to know what could cause your child so much mental and emotional pain that they thought dying was better than living?

I didn't want to know, so I didn't ask. I was scared of putting the thought back into her head, so I stayed silent.

A silence that lasted for 23 years.

Then, on Saturday, August the 3rd, 2019, Stephanie, now 37, breaks the silence.

The morning of her talk is sunny and already hot. The hotel is on the outskirts of Sarasota, FL. I walk into the conference room and greet the 12 speakers I've trained to deliver **"Messages That Matter."**

The videographer sets up, the mic and projector work, and the audience take their seats. Stephanie is nervous and excited - you know that state you get into right before you give a talk. She looks amazing in her dark blouse and flowery skirt with her hair pulled back in combs. I'm super proud of my daughter.

She's first up on the speaker's roster. The lights dim.

"Everyone, please help me welcome Stephanie Ashton!"

Stephanie walks confidently to the front of the room and shakes my hand.

She opens with: *"3,000 teens attempt to take their own lives every day in the US.*

In the back of the room, I'm stunned – twice . . . first because I have no idea the number is that high and second because I have no idea her topic is suicide.

Stephanie continues:

When I was 14, at the end of a bad day of shopping, I stood in my bathroom. The pain of not fitting into any clothes was just more proof that I didn't fit in anywhere. That pain was more than I could bear. I took a razor and cut into my left arm, trying to end the pain . . . and my life."

I'm in disbelief at Stephanie's big reveal. The blood drains from my face as Stephanie talks:

"It wasn't my only attempt. There were others. Outside of professional help, I've never really talked about it, not even with mom. Mom and I talked around it, but not about it. Too awkward. Too easy to avoid. Too painful.

Mom and I had other talks. We had "The Talk" about sex. We had "The Talk" about drugs. We had "The Talk" about alcohol. Then I went to college, on a dry campus . . . that means that the kegs were hidden in the showers in the girl's dorm.

Mom and I had "The Talk" about alcohol more than once.

But we never had "The Talk" about suicide. [pause]

I still struggle with suicidal thoughts."

In the back of the room, my heart sinks. I go from pale to bone cold . . .

For the first time I realize the struggles Stephanie faced alone because I didn't have the courage to break the silence and have "The Talk" about suicide.

Have you ever been hijacked by a bad memory?

Only my 30 years of stress management training keeps me from crawling into a corner and bawling.

Stephanie winds up her talk with:

"On my suicide-avoidant journey, I've learned tons of coping skills. Now, I want to help teens learn these skills before they need them. Yes, BEFORE they need them."

There's not a dry eye in the room, including mine.

The audience gives her a standing ovation. Some rush up to hug her and thank her for being so willing, so vulnerable, so brave.

I'm frozen in the back of the room, torn between pride for her bravery and guilt and shame for my cowardice.

Then it hit me . . . **3,000** teens attempt to end their lives every day . . .

This means every day **6,000** parents start to live the guilt-nightmare . . .

This means every day, over **20,000** grandparents, aunts, uncles, brothers, and sisters start to live the guilt-nightmare...

This means every day, **100s of 1,000s** of classmates, teachers, boyfriends, girlfriends and neighbors start to live the guilt-nightmare that I'd lived.

All, probably just as blind-sided by it as I had been.

Then I wondered, what if Stephanie was right and the key to stopping teen suicide could be as simple as having The Talk about suicide BEFORE it's needed. Before your teen struggles with suicidal thoughts.

This is the link that's been missing! Something so simple and obvious that professionals have tripped over it. Simple and obvious, like putting wheels on luggage or putting ketchup in squeezable bottles. Simple and obvious.

After the event, Stephanie and I decide to work together. Who knew that was possible?

Together with her sisters, we co-founded the Teen Suicide Prevention Society.

Our research taught us that teen suicide prevention is not about intervention, it's not about "at-risk" anyone, and it's NOT about looking for signs. Parents won't see the signs, even if there are some.

It's not your fault. Our brains naturally filter out what doesn't match our belief that "my child's OK."

That's why we say: Pre-vention means having "The Talk" about suicide BEFORE you think they need it.

We started teaching – moms, dads, grandparents, aunts, uncles, teachers, and friends – how to have The Talk about suicide.

The Talk about suicide is a planned, science-based talk. It has a short, simple guide based on how the teen brain really works. A guide designed to save you from the guilt-nightmare. A guide that tells you when intervention is needed. A guide that builds emotional resiliency, in both the teen and you.

Here's our 4-step guide for having "The Talk About Suicide:"

Please use the questions exactly as they appear. They are written in precise, neutral language for a reason.

Step 1:

Invite your teen to talk one-on-one and ask: "*Have you heard about the rise in teen suicides?*"

Take a deep breath and just listen.

Step 2:

Ask your teen: "Do you have a friend who's tried or died?"

Take a deep breath and just listen.

If they have a "friend story" please resist the temptation to try and make them feel better. Simply listen and continue.

Step 3:

Ask your teen: "Have you ever thought of leaving that way?"

Simply listen. A "Yes" to this question is NOT a red flag. It's a chance for them to feel heard and not judged. Simply listen and continue.

Step 4:

Ask your teen: "What are your reasons for staying?" "Why stay?"

Ask: "What else?"

Keep them talking about their reasons for staying. This is where the change happens. Celebrate every reason they give you and only offer your own reasons if they ask. Let this be your chance to discover what's meaningful to them.

NOTE:

If your teen has thoughts of leaving and **does not have any** reasons for staying, **STAY WITH THEM** and call 911*.

*Oh, they'll hate you for it AND you might save their life. One step down from calling 911 is calling a suicide or crisis intervention hotline.

In the USA, dial: 988 or 1-800-273-8255

It's often easier to talk with a stranger than with someone who might know the possible players in our pain.

Once you've asked and listened to all 4 Questions, share with your teen your "Have 'The Talk' Story." Share with them how (nervous, scared, excited) you were before having the talk. Share with them how grateful you are that they stayed. Offer them mindset tools (see below.) Plan time to use the tools together.

Our students share their stories with us.

Like Raphael who works with underprivileged teenage girls. He's shared that having "The Talk" about suicide has saved 16 lives so far.

Tammy had "The Talk" about suicide with her troubled son. They cried together. He accepted professional help. It doesn't matter that her son is grown and has a child of his own, it only matters that Tammy was willing to use the guide and have "The Talk."

Both Tammy and Raphael came to the Teen Suicide Prevention Society looking for help to talk about the hard things: Suicide, Bullying, Negative Thinking, Self-Sabotage, Dropping Out, Failing Classes, etc. What they found was FUN.

That's right, at the Teen Suicide Prevention Society ("TSPS") a.k.a.: "Teaspoons," we get that suicide is certainly serious and we believe that suicide prevention, pure prevention, can be seriously fun. We have amazing "neuro-gamified" card decks that teach emotional intelligence to kids as young as three years old, and we have computerized "vision-boards-on-steroids" for getting customized mood-boosting, affirmative statements past the critical thinking parts of your brain, we also have free and anonymous mental health assessments for depression and anxiety.

We're on a mission to make teen suicide a thing of the past.

We hope you'll join us.

Be prepared, you'll start with the fun stuff. You'll find out your personal "Know, Like, and Trust Factor." This assessment is super fun because it's all about what's so good about you.

Please continue to read this book and share your stories with us.

It's your turn . . .
Don't wait.
Break the silence.
Have "The Talk."

Table Of Contents

A Few Words from Mike Jones

The creator of the Make It A Great Day Concept

First, and foremost, I want to thank Jackie Simmons, my book success coach and publisher. Without you this project would most likely still be on a shelf somewhere. For more than a few reasons I value your friendship more than you know.

To all the teachers out there, no one can imagine the level of passion and commitment you have for your chosen profession. I've been blessed to have a couple in my family and call a couple more good friends.

To all the co-authors in this book, thank you for stepping up. You are truly special people. I can't tell you how many people were asked to be a part of this project; I deeply appreciate your time and you sharing your words of wisdom on how everyone can Make It A Great Day.

To the one that hears my prayers. I may not visit your house very often, but I appreciate your guidance. I know you're with me always on my walk. There's been more than once I've thought how easy it would be to "take the easy way out." Then you remind me this 3rd rock from the sun has so many miracles all around us. Every day Is a Great Day.

Lastly, I'd like to acknowledge my kids: Bryson, Danni, Nick, Michael, Marrisa, and Kimi. Thinking of you makes me smile.

A Few Words from Jackie Simmons
Co-founder of the Teen Suicide Prevention Society

When Mike Jones shared this concept of a book of inspirational stories for teens, I thought, "What a great idea, this will be easy," but dozens of phone calls, hundreds of emails, multiple moving deadlines, and 15 months later, "easy" is not the word I would use to describe compiling this book.

Other things kept getting in the way. My "busy-ness" kept me from just getting it done (see the chapter on Elephants.)

It took a 7-minute talk on the rise in teen suicide rates to cut through all the distractions, time constraints, and excuses.

I want to acknowledge all the authors, first-readers, members of the Make A Difference Book Launch Lounge, hand-holders (Nadine Vernon), editors and designers (Mark Walzer, Lily Erdy, and Lil Barcaski), my publisher Becky Norwood for sticking with this project, and my daughters for believing that it is the right time to #breakthesilence on teen suicide and start "'The Talks' that Save Lives."

To learn how you too can have the talks that save lives, visit:

www.TeenSuicidePreventionSociety.com

1

And Then There Were Elephants

by Jackie Simmons

The "Elephant in the Room" metaphor is often used to describe something obvious to others that we usually cannot see. The "Elephant in the Room" is whatever holds us back, makes us sad, keeps us frustrated, or pisses us off.

Are you good at spotting other people's elephants? What about your own?

My Elephant showed up and was sitting on my phone, so I couldn't make sales calls, and he distracted me so that I couldn't focus or finish projects. My Elephant's name was "Enthusiastic."

Now, don't get me wrong, being enthusiastic is a great source of inspiration and energy. It's one of the most attractive emotions you can wear. But, for me, being enthusiastic had become a problem.

See, I was enthusiastic about whatever the person I was with was into. It felt so good to be enthusiastic that I would join into their dream or vision and often abandon my own in the process.

If there was any way that I could help or participate, I couldn't say "No" without feeling guilty, so I was saying "Yes," often . . .

If I couldn't say "No" guilt free, then along came Enthusiastic, the Elephant, wearing a bright-colored t-shirt with a big, bold "YES" embroidered on it and I'd be off and running on another venture.

The problem was that I couldn't get anything done on my own projects.

I networked a lot to grow my business, so I was constantly hearing about what other people were pursuing . . . there was always something else to say an Enthusiastic "Yes" to.

No one really knew what my business was about because I was always talking about the latest thing that I had said "Yes" to. I was excited and exciting to be around. I was also secretly frustrated that I wasn't making any progress on my own stuff.

Riding Enthusiastic the Elephant, saying "Yes" to anything that wasn't a guilt-free "No" was exhausting and expensive. I was popular, and broke.

I pondered and tried to imagine what the problem was, what my Elephant looked like. That's when I realized that I wasn't just riding one Elephant, I was riding two.

In my mind I could see them clearly. There was "Enthusiastic," with a bold "YES" embroidered on his t-shirt and the second Elephant was: "Guilt Free," and Guilt Free was wearing a t-shirt embroidered with a bright "NO."

Whenever there was an opportunity, Guilt Free was always first in the room and if I couldn't say "NO" to a project guilt free, Enthusiastic was right there with that bold "YES" and off I went, enthusiastically pursuing yet another project.

It was making me crazy. I started to imagine that the Elephants were watching me, always looking for more opportunities to play.

As I said "Yes" to more and more projects, I got less and less done. I grumped around and fussed at my invisible companions and then laughed at myself for dreaming up Elephants.

I took a break and imagined what life would be like if my Elephants could help me focus instead of helping me create more distractions.

I think the Elephants must have been imagining, too.

I went back into my office and started reading emails; sure enough, another offer appeared, and I couldn't find a way to say "No" to it guilt free, so I started to say "Yes," and then the Elephants arrived and unlike before, this time I could see them.

The first elephant in the room was still Guilt Free, but he wasn't looking for me to be able to say a guilt-free "NO," this time he was looking to see if I could say a guilt-free "YES" because he was wearing a new t-shirt and this one had a big, bold "YES" on it.

Well, that's different. I mean, there's no way I could say "Yes" to the offer guilt free because saying "Yes" would mean that I didn't have time to work on the projects I'd already started.

OH! That was a new thought and right on Guilt Free's heels was Enthusiastic, also with a new t-shirt. This one had a big, bright "NO" on it!

Woo-hoo, a new rule - if an offer's not a guilt-free "Yes," then it's automatically an enthusiastic "No!"

I was still riding Elephants, but now I was also productive! I zipped through my emails and enthusiastically said "No!" to everything that wasn't a guilt-free "Yes." Even networking, I was now enthusiastically saying "No" to everything that would have distracted me before.

Dressed appropriately, Guilt Free and Enthusiastic became my "Elephants of Productivity" and you're welcome to ride them whenever you want.

Just don't let them change t-shirts!

2

Animals As Teachers and Healers!

by Wendy Cooper, MSW

Animal Communication (AC) is an exchange of thoughts and feelings between animals and other animals, or animals and people, through the mind instead of the five senses. AC connects you with animals, telepathically, accessing their wisdom about them and about you.

AC can give you a new understanding of your pet's needs and preferences and offer you confidence about, and competence with your daily life challenges. AC takes you to a meditative state of mind. That, alone, can help to improve your mood, but it also gives you the chance to open up to great possibilities about your life! Human ability to do AC is hard-wired and natural. It does take practice to get your 'spiritual muscles' in shape. Your pet wants to assist you when you are in need and will appreciate your efforts to connect via the universal language of telepathy.

What drew me to AC? Zsa Zsa, my 5-pound Maltese, was a sick puppy. After two years of holistic and regular vet care, one of my vets suggested that I use an animal communicator. My response was, "An animal what?" I needed to try three animal communicators to truly believe in its validity.

Each one was slightly different, but all gave me similar data. They told me many things but, mainly that Zsa Zsa was grieving because she was used to serving clients in my psychotherapy practice. I had recently closed the practice to move on to a different career.

They said that I should take her to lots of places so that she could bring joy and lightness to the world. Zsa Zsa completely shifted as I completed my assignment! Everyone smiled at the sight of her. Even macho men would melt when they met Zsa Zsa.

Subsequently, I regularly used animal communicators for Zsa Zsa and even took classes to learn to do AC myself. I found it especially helpful when she was age 11 and preparing to transition. Die, that is. The AC was incredibly useful because I learned what Zsa Zsa needed during this difficult time. Moreover, it assisted me to understand death in a completely different way, and to receive personal messages directly from Zsa Zsa about my own life path.

Of course I grieved, but the AC gave me solace in the most amazing way. It also helped me immensely on my own life journey. This personal experience is why most of my AC practice revolves around helping people and animals before, during, and after their pet's transition. (For more about Zsa Zsa's story, go to www.AnimalCommunication.biz)

How do you do AC? Take a few deep breaths to get centered in your body. As you look at a regular photo of your pet, gaze into its eyes and call its name three times (out loud or silently) as you think about your pet to get his/her attention, energetically. Get very quiet and listen because pets usually want to telepathically talk first. You will start to access information from various parts of your brain; but think of those messages in terms of your five senses. You may (in your mind) hear words or see pictures.

You may get a feeling in your body, such as an emotion or a physical sensation. You may experience a smell or start salivating if your pet wants to give you food requests! For some people, it is easiest to keep staring at the photo and for others, it is best to close the eyes to keep listening deeply.

As you are still focused on your pet, notice your next thought because the data can be similar to a computer download, where it just comes to you. Listen to all your animal 'says' before asking any questions. Take a few notes so you remember your pet's requests. Then ask a specific question about the pet's preferences or about a personal issue of your own.

Again, be silent and listen until you stop receiving data. Once complete, always thank your pet for its help. If you make a promise to your pet while doing AC, please keep your promise! For instance, if you agree to give him/her a new kind of treat, follow through. That will build trust between you and your pet on many levels. You can regularly practice for fun and in order to get better and better with your AC skills.

Feel free to practice with wild animals or animals in captivity, such as in zoos and aquariums! Always ask permission before using AC with an animal who has a human companion. And, if the human says yes, then ask if there is anything that they would not want to know so that you are being respectful to the human.

We all experience 'monkey mind' where our thoughts are racing. Be patient because it can take practice to get those spiritual muscles in shape. Doing AC encourages and assists us to slow down and be open to answers.

Your personal style: All of us have an easiest, most natural way of receiving data. (Again, think of your five senses.) Personally, it is simplest for me to 'hear' the data, but, because I have practiced so much, I also receive lots of images in my mind, feelings in my body, and a gut feeling about what the animal is 'saying.' Play with receiving messages in these different ways.

The animals like to answer your call, so be persistent as you pay attention to their messages! Doing regular meditation is another way to get your spiritual muscle in shape so that you can get better at receiving messages from animals. Listen with your heart instead of your ears!

How do you know when it is real? You won't always know when it's real. Look for proof via your everyday life with your pet and in your life, but don't depend on it. Notice whether the information from your pet is helpful to you AND if it feels right. Know that the animal's voice is never shaming or mean. Stay open to your pet's humor! They love it when you laugh. People may discount your AC messages simply because they do not understand AC. YOU can still believe!

What about animal totems? When you see, think, or dream about a kind of animal, (especially repeatedly) you can do AC to receive personal messages for your life path. You can tune into a specific animal species. Say pigs keep coming to you in movies, books, or in your daily life. Just say "pig, pig, pig" as a way of doing AC with the pig totem. Moreover, there are lots of internet links to assist you about the symbolism of specific animals. This website is one of my favorites:

www.whats-your-sign.com/animal-totems.html.

Animal Communication is a quick, fun way to receive answers and a great way to be at your best!

3

Become the Person You Want to Be

by Lil Barcaski

"Don't quit your day job" is basically what my father told me at age twenty when I gave him the first four chapters of the novel I was writing. Dad was a successful writer, but his genre was textbooks. He got paid to write, so I took his review of my work to heart and left my concept of becoming a professional writer in the dust.

I am an artist at heart. I continued to play music, learned the art of cooking, and became a success in both of those areas.

But I didn't write.

Twenty years later, when I met the woman that would become my wife, and eventually my ex-wife, I was thrust back into the world of writing. She was an up-and-coming fantasy writer and we talked about writing, went to writing conventions and conferences, and suddenly the idea of writing began to once again appeal to me.

But I was lousy at it.

I started working on a novel that we conceived of on a trip to the Florida Keys. We mapped out the concept, the characters, the story, and plot. I started on Chapter One.

"Okay," she said after reading it. "It's a good start, but you need to be more succinct; you need to add more dialogue and less exposition."

"Exposition?" I asked quizzically.

"Thread the story out through dialogue; and it has to feel natural. Don't just tell the reader what's happening. Let the reader experience what's happening. Bring them into the story."

I rewrote the chapter and several more.

"Now, you're on track," she said. "And your dialogue is excellent."

I never finished that novel. What I did finish was a play. And then another, and another. And those plays were chosen for large play festivals. My newest play is being produced at a very important festival in Orlando, Florida.

Later, I was introduced to the concept of ghostwriting. I got hired to write blogs for companies who would put the owner's name on the blog I wrote. Then I wrote a business book for a client; then another and another.

"I want to write my memoir. Can you help me with that?" "I have an idea for a novel, but I don't write well. Can you write it for me?"

"I would like a writing coach to get me on track with my writing. Are you available for that?"

Yes, yes, and yes!

Now, I get paid more than $15,000 a book when I ghostwrite. I write fiction books, business books, memoirs, biographies. My name is on many books as the author, co-author, or editor. I even own a publishing company.

It took me 20 years to begin the first steps on the path I should probably have been on in college. Did I do other things that were satisfying and successful? Yes. But I let the words of my father delay the one thing I was actually meant to do.

There are lots of things you're probably capable of doing. There are skills you have that can make you money. But the thing that makes you happy and makes enough money to live the lifestyle you choose is the career that will call you and make you feel successful.

Don't let anyone burst your balloon. Don't let anyone discourage you from becoming the person you want to be.

Even if you downright suck at the thing you want to do, you can learn to be better. You can, in fact, learn to be great at it. You may have certain God-given skills. Maybe you're a great athlete or have a terrific singing voice. Maybe those talents make you happy and will lead to a wonderful career. But sometimes it's the thing we aren't great at, but hunger to be GREAT at, that makes us happy.

Don't give up. Find a teacher, a mentor, someone who can guide you and help you get there. Read books, watch YouTube videos. Everything you want to learn is probably in a video somewhere on YouTube.

Don't give up on your idea of who or what you can be. Contribute to the world. Bring your joy and drive to the things that you feel passionate about. Explore every possibility.

I'll tell you a secret. They say: "Life is Short." That's a lie.

Life is Long! You have time, and time is a great thing to have. So, if someone tells you "Don't quit your day job!" tell them what I should have told my father: "I don't need a day job. I'm going to be a writer."

4

Brain Food
by Nadine Vernon

Changing your focus is often hard but not impossible.

Retraining one's mindset just takes practice. Each exercise below represents a different "food group" for your brain.

The goal is to have a balanced diet. Do each exercise below and share your answers with a friend. All types of food, even brain food, digest better when shared.

1. What's In a Word?

Turn the word HATE into LOVE in four steps by changing only ONE LETTER as you move to the next line. Each line must contain a real word.

HATE

— — — —

— — — —

— — — —

LOVE

2. Who's Who?

Miss Self-Esteem, Mr. Positivity, and Mr. Self-Worth are speaking to one another. Each holds one notecard labeled with either the word "Self-Esteem," "Positivity," or "Self-Worth."

Mr. Positivity says, "Did you see that each of us is holding a different notecard than our name?"

The person holding the Self-Worth card exclaims, "Very true, Mr. Positivity!"

With just the information above, discover who's holding the Self-Esteem notecard. Did you get all three people matched with their cards?

3. Empowering You.

Create a silhouette of your head or hand. Cut empowering words from magazines and paste them in your silhouette. Use this collage as a reminder of who you are and who you can strive to be.

4. Love is in The Air

Name ten songs that have LOVE in the title.

1. _____

2. _____

3. _____

4. _____

5. _____

6. _____

7. _____

8. _____

9. _____

10. _____

5. Grow Your Gratitude

Each week draw a "Gratitude Tree." Every day, label at least one leaf with something you are grateful for. Each leaf should be uniquely labeled without repeats. Compare your trees at the end of the month.

6. Brain Change

Your subconscious mind can create a new mindset. It's possible to train our brains to accept a new belief with positive affirmations, meditations, and focused concentration. Alpha brain waves, present in deep relaxation, contribute to this retraining.

a. Write a short affirmation: I am worthy, I am beautiful, I am lovable, I am . . .

b. Find a quiet spot.

c. Close your eyes. Take slow, deep breaths.

d. Now repeat your affirmation in a whisper, over and over for five minutes.

e. Repeat daily.

7. What's Worth Keeping?

Remove a letter and rearrange the remaining letters to make a new word until only a one-letter word remains. Each line must contain a real word.

D I G E S T

___ ___ ___ ___ ___

___ ___ ___ ___

___ ___ ___

___ ___

___

8. Stuck in The Middle?

Each 4-letter word is the middle of a larger word. Fill in the blanks to create the bigger word.

___ ___ J U S T ___ ___
___ ___ P E N D ___ ___
___ ___ T I R E ___ ___
___ ___ A N T I ___ ___
___ ___ S E A R ___ ___

9. Mixed Values?

Unscramble the letters to create words.

PHAYP   MASEOWE

VREBA   TINDOCFEN

OTNSGR   RENLUWFOD

GOINVL   UGREOCA

"We are our choices."

— *Jean-Paul Sartre*

You get to choose the words that you use; choose wisely.

5

Don't Hold Back

by Jeannette Bridoux

You matter.

Your worth, your value, and your importance don't rely on how many Instagram likes you have . . .

How many followers . . .

Or how many friends you have at school.

Your value is inside of you. It's not something anyone can ever take away or give. It's something you were born with. From the moment you were conceived, you had value.

Before you joined a sports team, won an award, or got your first boyfriend or girlfriend. No external thing will ever define your greatness and value. Not where you grow up, not how much your parents make, or even if you don't have parents.

These are the words I wish someone would've told me at your age. Growing up, I was in constant need of approval.

From teachers, my parents, and my friends. It drove all my decisions. I chose the popular friends who weren't really my friends. I chose to do things that they did because they did them. I chose to follow the crowd because that was acceptable.

While I may have been getting the approval I wanted at school, I was lonely inside. No one told me that when you follow the crowd, you end up on a path you weren't meant to be on.

In a place you weren't meant to be. With people you weren't meant to be with. Doing something you weren't meant to do. Being someone, you weren't meant to be.

That's what happened to me. Because I didn't understand my value and worth. I saw myself as unwanted, unimportant, and unworthy. Because I was looking at what everyone else had and everything I didn't.

I thought to be important, your parents had to drive an Escalade.

I thought to be important, I had to be a cheerleader.

I thought to be important, I had to be good at sports.

So, as I didn't have any of those things, I thought I must not be important or have any value. By focusing on what

I didn't have and what others had, I missed out on seeing what amazing gifts, talents I had inside me all along. Because I felt like I didn't have value or importance, I went looking for it.

I tried finding it in…

Boys
Parties
Awards
Titles

But I didn't find significance or belonging, I found depression. I struggled with it for years. I hid my emotions and played off like everything was ok.

Until one day, many years later, I hit my breaking point. I finally realized where my significance really was . . . inside of me. I finally saw that my voice and my ideas mattered because I mattered. I discovered that I am here for a reason, and I found my purpose. I found it when I stopped being what everyone else wanted me to be.

When I stopped looking around at what other people valued and started discovering my own values. I found my purpose when I was honest with myself about what I really wanted, even if it was scary or felt impossible.

Because here's the thing, nothing is impossible. You are limitless.

It's our ideas and our perception of ourselves and our reality that holds us back from living the life WE were meant to live. Not the beliefs or ideas that others have for our lives.

Why should we let anyone, or anything, create limits for us?

It's when we stop looking on the outside and turn inside that we discover our true self without judgement or limitations.

Embracing that, is where you find your significance and value.

And it's always been there.

So, how can you make today a great day?

Stop looking around to decide who you are and your values. Be the rebel who steps out and does something that's uniquely you - not a copycat version of someone else.

Determine your own values and voice and stand for them.

Don't let others shake you with their own opinions and let them project their values on you. It's ok to be different.

Know you are valuable no matter what job you get, what college you go to, who your parents are, or what the world says is possible for you.

You are limitless and you have limitless potential. Practice loving and appreciating all the things that make you who you are. Shoot for the stars, and don't let the limits people place on themselves place limits on you.

You are here for a purpose.

It's OK to not know exactly what it is yet, but if you follow your heart, your values, and your limitless potential, you will find yourself on the path to your purpose. Know that every challenge you face along the way is preparing you for your next victory, and getting you closer to your destiny.

You have the power to make a difference, **don't hold back.**

6
Even With Dog Turds!
by Valerie LaBoy

Working in real estate can be a lot of fun and yet frustrating at times. In real estate, there are no regular paychecks, only commissions that come once a sale is finalized. I might work with someone for months to help them sell their home, then complications arise when buyers, agents, inspectors, and lenders become involved. My job is to keep the variables under control and to keep everyone calm and focused on the goal, which is to sell the home.

Sometimes sellers urgently need to sell – which puts extra stress on me to move the home quickly. This was the case with a woman I'll call April. She was a friend who needed surgery and needed to move back to Pennsylvania where family could help her.

Arriving at April's home, I was greeted by five little dogs lunging at the door as though they would break right through it. I took out my little bag of biscuits that I always carry and waited for April. "Hello, hello!" she said, smiling. "Don't mind my fur babies, they always carry on so." As the door opened, a wall of stench slammed into my face, and I thought I'd pass out. The carpet had big yellow and brown stains and little turds in several places.

April said that the dogs had "accidents" sometimes. I really wanted to turn around and walk out – but I had no other listings and needed the commission that would come when (and if) this home sold.

I called an odor removal service who wanted $3000 to wash the walls and baseboards with a bleach solution, tear out the carpeting, and clean the air conditioning ducts; with no guarantee it would work. April did not have the money and said she would clean it herself. She tried, but the odor was still there.

I hosted open house events with windows wide open, used candles and room fresheners, and advertised the house. When other realtors brought buyers, everyone said the same thing – nice house, awful smell. But soon, we received an offer to purchase!

I was shocked. The buyers couldn't smell it at all! They loved the layout and the fenced yard and were looking forward to tearing up the carpet and tiling the floors. So, they bought the home and moved in within the month.

Lesson learned:

> You never know.
> Do your best and don't get discouraged!

7

Getting to the Top of the Hill
by Cody Dakota Wooten

I stood at the bottom of the hill looking up, thinking to myself… what had gone wrong? What was so wrong with me that led to what I saw at this moment? My heart sank. I felt lost. All hope vanished in an instant. What was I seeing?

About five weeks prior, I was driving with my fiancée. I had just finished meeting her family for the first time. Everything felt perfect. After we were back on the road to meet my family halfway across the country, something felt wrong though, and I didn't know what it was until . . .

She asked for us to pull over. She told me that she needed to break off our engagement without telling me why. She told me that she still loved me and wanted to stay with me, just not engaged. I wanted to believe that was true.

Three weeks prior, we were in the laundry room. She told me that she couldn't do it any longer, that she needed to break the relationship. Again, she wouldn't give me any reason why. She wouldn't tell me what I did wrong, just that it needed to end.

One week prior, I was trying to figure out what I could do to fix our relationship, trying to rationalize what went wrong, where things went wrong. I needed the support of my best friend and roommate, the only other person I was really close to other than her.

The person I had helped through the toughest of times, who had cried on my shoulder, who I had spent years of my life with. He never came home that night.

Now, I'm looking up the hill to see my ex-fiancée hand-in-hand with my best friend and roommate, as if they were the only two people in the world . . .

How did this happen? What did I do so wrong that the two people I trusted most would completely turn their backs on me like this? How could the two people I thought I was going to spend the rest of my life with suddenly cut me out as if I didn't exist?

All of these questions and more passed through my mind over the next year, and I fell into a deeper and deeper depression.

I remember some days I would walk into my room, look straight out the window in front of me on the third floor we lived on and think, "The window isn't that strong . . . if I were to do a light jog, go headfirst, straight down into the cement below . . . " That thought went through my mind many times during this period, and others as well, but I never actually attempted my own suicide.

What prevented me from starting that jog? How did I overcome my depression? How did I turn my life around and make it even better? How did I find new love, create stronger friendships, start my own business, get nominated for the "Extraordinarian Award," and be asked to join the Forbes Coaches Council in less than five years?

It all happened because I began to focus on what I call L.I.F.E.

I believe that L.I.F.E. is the key to overcoming all the problems we face in the world, and it is definitely what helped me turn my world around.

L – stands for Legacy

I thought about what I wanted people to say about me when I died. I didn't want them to say, "Oh, he had so much potential, but he didn't amount to much and died a hermit." NO! I wanted people to look up to me. I wanted them to be amazed at the things I accomplished. I wanted them to say, "Wow! If he could do it, why couldn't I?"

I – stands for Impact
I had to look at my life and determine what talents and abilities I had that I could utilize to change peoples' lives, to change the world.

F – stands for Flow
Flow is a state of consciousness which is characterized by a feeling of selflessness (kind of like being "one" with everything occurring around you, and self-criticism disappears), timelessness, effortlessness, and richness. For me, I found these in having great conversations with new friends I made, playing lacrosse, and doing martial arts.

E – stands for Empowerment
I needed to search for what in my life left me feeling stronger, more confident, emancipated, unshackled.

What we focus on, we find more of,
and that's what I did.
What will you focus on for your L.I.F.E.?

8

Hairy Legs
by Shauna E. VanderHoek

Eighth grade was horrid!

My clothes were second-hand: shabby and out of style. My skirt was too long. And my Mom wouldn't let me shave my legs until I turned 16.

A boy I had a crush on had just pointed at me and snickered to his friend, "Look at those hairy legs."

I wanted the ground to swallow me up. Just let me out of here!

Have you ever felt that way?

I didn't know then how to move on from the hurt and shame, so I was stuck in it for years. But I did make it through. In retrospect, I slowly crawled up something called "the emotional scale" (as described in Hawkins book, Power vs. Force).

I started at the bottom end of the emotional scale in shame – ashamed of my appearance.

Apathy:

Within a few days, I'd decided my "crush" wasn't the guy I'd thought he was. I dropped my crush. (Apathy is upscale from shame!)

Next was Fear:

What if I would always be made fun of?

Then Desire:

I craved acceptance.

Anger (even higher on the emotional scale) was the toughest. I had been taught that anger was bad, but stuffing it kept me from rising to the higher emotions like pride, willingness, and acceptance.

Finally – regardless that it was "bad"– I got angry about how I'd been treated.

Finally, I could move on.

Hate the way you feel?
Climb the emotional scale.

9

How to do an Impossible Task

by Ken Streater

When faced with an "impossible" task, take five minutes to list five things you have already handled or overcome in your life. When we remind ourselves that we have dealt well with many challenges in the past, we feel better about the chances of overcoming more challenges in the future. Remembering and saluting what you have successfully faced gives you more strength to get through another task.

Now, let's make this idea interactive. I encourage you to write down five things you have effectively handled or overcome in your life. Raised kids? Check. Fought through a serious illness? Write it down. Worked your way up a career ladder despite missing rungs? Give yourself credit. Rebounded from a broken heart? Record that.

At one point in my life, I spent 20 or more hours a day for eight straight months lying in bed or on the floor. I had ruptured a couple of disks in my back from years of bodily abuse as a river guide and for disregarding early warning signs to take care of my lower back. The result was stabbing nerve pain down my right leg that prevented me from standing or sitting for more than a few minutes at a time. It felt like a freight train was running back and forth over my leg.

My days consisted of making myself something to eat, going to the bathroom, taking half-a-block walks, and looking at the ceiling.

As a thirty-something, I was distraught by the belief that this would be my life, forever. Until, gradually, I got better. Now I use this period as a reminder of what is possible even when you feel like there is no point in trying or going on. I also know this challenge pales in comparison to what far too many others in the world have to endure in the form of severe physical challenges or deep emotional scars.

Simply put, you and I and others have overcome challenges that could have sent us spinning down, down, down - never to get back up. But we got back up. The problem is we often forget just how talented, resilient, focused, determined, and capable we are. And we most often forget this when we need it the most — when we need to pull it together, find another way, and lift ourselves up off the mat, when we need to elevate.

If you have not written down your list of five things, please do it now. I'll wait:

1. _____

2. _____

3. _____

4. _____

5. _____

Thanks. Now, take out your phone and snap a photo of this. The next time you are wondering if you are going to make it, if another step looks to be one too many to take, look at this list. Carry it with you to hold in your heart, to honor all that you have been through, and to remember the gift that it is to you now.

This reflection will change your perspective about what you face today. It is your past overcoming – and the reminder of the strengths that you have – that form your ability to rise above or push through the next challenges you will face.

(excerpt from: *Be The Good: Becoming A Force For A Better World*)

10

I Shouldn't Be Here

by Stephanie Ashton

Hot tears roll down my face as I stare at the papers scattered across my desk. I'm breathing faster and faster as panic sets in. This essay has to be perfect. My future depends on it!

I'm staring blankly at college applications, overwhelmed and absolutely unable to write a single word for my admission essays.

"This is supposed to be fun. You can do this. Applying for college is an exciting, freeing time. This is when I'm supposed to launch myself into the world, look out here comes Stephanie!"

Instead, I'm a hot mess as all too familiar thoughts pour into my head: "Why am I even trying? I'm just going to get rejected anyways. No school is going to be interested in me. Nothing I have to say is going to be of interest to anyone. This is pointless, an exercise in futility. It's useless,

I'm useless. I'm worthless. I'm not good enough to go to college. I'm just going to fail. I'm not smart enough for this."

The tears start coming faster and faster. My eyes are burning from them, and I can no longer see the papers in front of me. I want to give up, make the pain stop. My chest feels like it's bursting from the pain. What can I do to make this pain go away? I hurt so incredibly much inside. Maybe if I hurt on the outside, I won't hurt so much inside?

No. Been there, done that.

I can't catch my breath. Why can't I breathe? I sob harder. The thoughts turn darker, and I know what's coming next: "Nobody loves me. Nobody cares. It wouldn't be the end of the world if something were to happen to me. Maybe, maybe I don't belong here on this planet. Life would be a lot easier on mom. I'm such a burden to her, if I were dead, she would be free of me. Wouldn't that be a good thing? My sisters can't stand me so what's the point in staying in their lives? I shouldn't be here. I shouldn't be alive."

That's it! That's the title for my essay - "I Shouldn't Be Here." No. No, that won't work. I haven't survived a tragedy or illness or anything. They'll laugh at me if I write about this. Besides, who cares? Nobody wants to hear me whine or complain. Nobody will listen. I sigh, brace myself, and begin writing a boring, safe, generic essay.

I was sixteen, on medication, seeing a psychiatrist, seeing a therapist, and still suicidal. I'd been diagnosed with major depression when I was fourteen and been in treatment since then. My parents, bless them, sent me to the same doctor and therapist that one of them was already seeing and I didn't feel comfortable opening up. I didn't speak up. To anyone. I didn't know that it was OK to say that I was not OK, even while I was under treatment. Even though my parents were paying these people to listen to me I was convinced that they couldn't possibly care about someone as damaged as me. I thought there was something wrong with me, that I couldn't be fixed.

Every day was like trudging through mud and muck because of the weight of depression. I did get accepted to college and I went to live in the dorms at seventeen. It wasn't long before I started experimenting with alcohol. Over the next several years I self-medicated with alcohol, drugs, and bad relationships. The alcohol and drugs numbed the noise in my head, and I thought they helped me function.

I thought I deserved the bad relationships. At 22, I had a mental breakdown and was hospitalized on a psych unit for a week. I dropped out of college and focused entirely on numbing out. Eight months later I was back on the psych unit, and I checked myself into rehab.

Over the next five years I had eleven more stays. I learned a lot on those units, and I honestly have some fond memories of some of them. For instance, during my first stay the nurses left a supply closet unlocked. Several of us took two wheelchairs out of the closet. We lined up in the longest hallway on the unit and started to have wheelchair races. We had so much fun racing down that hallway! We took turns who was pushing and who was sitting. The nurses let us get away with it for about ten minutes. I'm not sure why but I'm grateful they did. It felt good to goof off. It was a break from the seriousness of why we were there.

My recovery has taken a long time and I sought help lots of places. I got the right diagnosis when I was twenty-three, but I didn't find the right psychiatrist and therapist until I was twenty-eight.

It was during those five years that I was on and off the psych unit so much, absolutely determined to get well. I kept fighting.

Day in, day out. I lost count of the number of doctors and therapists I saw over those five years. I kept asking for help. There's absolutely no shame in asking for help; and if you don't get it the first time, keep asking! For me finding the right doctor and therapist was key. My psychiatrist is wonderful. She's trustworthy, she listens, she's thorough, and she's all about looking at both my mental health and physical health since I also deal with chronic health issues.

We go over my medications at every appointment, discuss new medical and social history, and decide if any changes to treatment are necessary.

My therapist was phenomenal. I saw him at least once a week for eight years.

That might sound excessive but for me it was exactly what I needed.

With him, I didn't need to put on a face. I could finally be honest and start to heal. I "graduated" last year but I know that therapy is always there for me if I need it. I've learned to never stop asking for help. There is no shame in it.

To be honest, for me, despite all the work I've done on psych units, in therapy and the work I continue to do with my psychiatrist and in twelve step recovery groups, the suicidal thoughts are never far away.

They actually visited me two days ago. They still sound the same: "There's something wrong with me, I shouldn't be here."

Here's the good news though: those thoughts are background noise now. They don't dominate my life. I have learned a variety of tools that help me to live joyfully with this background noise. When those thoughts came two days ago, I was able to recognize them for the noise that they were, I quickly took action to take care of myself and was able to end the day with a smile.

A few years ago, I didn't believe it was possible to live a happy, fulfilling life while still having suicidal thoughts. I thought it was an all or nothing thing – either I was "sick" with the thoughts, or I was "well" and free from them. Guess what?

I'm "well" and I live happily and joyfully with suicidal thoughts. I'm now on a mission to share with tweens, teens, and young adults the tools and tricks I've learned and developed. I want to make sure that they have the support and tools that I wish that I had when I was younger.

This has become my passion in life. So many people talk about mental health awareness, but few people talk solutions.

I don't think anyone else should have to struggle as long as it took me to learn how to thrive with suicidal thoughts.

I want you to know that no matter what you hear in your head, no matter what "depression" is telling you, you are worthy, you are loved, and you deserve a happy life.

Today, I live my life with a lot of laughter and a lot of joy, and you can, too.

If you need help with that, reach out.

11

It's All Inside of You
by Becky Scheliga

I'll never forget the day.

To anyone else, it looked like just another ordinary day. However, for me, it would forever be branded in my mind as the day where the pain became too much for me.

I had lived with depression for over a decade, and had certainly seen my fair share of bad days. This was different, though. The delicate balance of my past experiences that had been teetering like an ill-balanced house of cards, finally came crashing down. Every moment of abuse and betrayal and neglect lay around me in a chaos that felt far beyond mending. And even if it could be mended, I didn't have the energy to take on a project of that magnitude. Instead, I just wanted to toss the whole mess out. I committed to the decision and opened the bottle of pills I had been tightly gripping in my hand and bid the cruel world I had known goodbye.

I don't know about having your life flash before your eyes in those final moments, because, for me, it was the life that I was never going to live that I saw.

I saw all of these events and experiences that I was going to miss out on. After all, I was just shy of thirty and still had so many things in my mind that I would've liked to accomplish in my life. All of these thoughts, feelings, and emotions flashed by in seconds, although it felt like an eternity. I couldn't purge my regrets from my system fast enough.

After my near bout with death, and two weeks in a rehab center, I made this promise to myself that I wasn't going to let that happen to me again. I knew where my demons were hiding now, and I was going to eradicate them. At least this was my intention. Instead, it took almost five years to find medications that worked and a therapist I felt I could actually trust with my demons. And, by then, I was already sliding back down into a deep depression.

Despite my efforts of slaying the beast inside my mind, I was at the point of no return, again. I felt like a failure, and I felt like continuing my battle was utterly hopeless. After all, here I sat crying on another bathroom floor, looking at the wreck that was my life, and holding a bottle of pills, trying to understand the point of it all. It was in that moment that I heard this voice in my head. It was familiar to me, yet somehow foreign. It was telling me that

I still had work to do here. It kept telling me this over and over, until I realized where I knew this voice from. It was my own voice. Except it was the voice of the girl I had buried down deep underneath all the pain and shame I had been carrying around. It was the authentic, unapologetic, honest version of myself. That was a pivotal moment for me. It was the moment that changed everything.

To say that I turned my life around is an understatement. I'm a completely different person and have been free of my symptoms of depression for almost three full years now. That doesn't mean I'm some magical creature that doesn't have bad days, but my bad days are no longer defeating and debilitating. I decided to start my own business so I could help coach others through this process of changing their lives. It's now my mission to spread my message with anyone who will listen.

The message that you, and only you, are in control of your life and writing your own story.

Let me be the one to tell you that the light at the end of the tunnel doesn't exist. You are the light, and it doesn't only appear when you're at the end. It's always inside of you. I know there are things and people that are going to try and dim that light. Some might even succeed at times, but this doesn't make you weak, or any less of a person. I know so many people will tell you, "Just wait, it gets better." Honestly, the truth is that it does get better, but it's about making the choice to make it better.

If there is anything that I've learned from all of my trials and tribulations, it is that everything that you are searching for is already inside of you. Happiness, beauty, love, confidence, acceptance, the answers, you name it . . . you will never truly find these things outside of yourself. The moment that I listened to that voice inside of me, was the moment I realized that everything I had been looking for all this time, was buried deep inside of me. And I promise you, it is all inside of you, too.

So, I leave you with this. Just know that change is possible, and that you are capable of changing whatever you set your mind to. Do not shrink yourself to fit into someone else's box, do not stop chasing your dreams, and what lights you up inside, and do not ever forget how unbelievably amazing you are. There is someone out there that needs you, and no one else, and who needs to hear your voice, and no one else's. Don't you ever give up on yourself and the life you are meant for in this world.

12

Leaving Shouldville
by Jackie Simmons

Shouldville is a weird little town that has lots of places to live and very few reasons to live there.

In Shouldville, people hang out and talk about all their reasons for not moving out. After all, most families have been living in Shouldville for generations – sharing lots of shame and blame and very little happiness.

In fact, happiness is reserved for the people who leave on vacation to visit their "Happy Place." People who try to bring their happy place back with them to Shouldville are shunned. It's OK to have a memento or two that you talk about with nostalgia, or even a sense of sadness, but actively bringing your happy place into Shouldville gets you ostracized.

For me, vacationing in my Happy Place didn't happen very often, most of my days were spent in Shouldville, participating in "should-fests." Should-fests are the main activity of Shouldville residents ("Shouldees").

You can spot a "Shouldee" by their tendency to start should-fests. A should-fest is any conversation with yourself or others that starts with "I should" or "They should."

Should-fests often become competitions to see who can make the other person (or yourself) feel the worst. It starts with a simple: "I should've known better." or "They shouldn't have done that."

In my home it often starts with "What made you think that was a good idea?" and rapidly escalates into a full-out should-slinging contest.

Should-slinging contests happen often in the lower end of Shouldville where I was raised, and I wanted no part of it. I dreamed of moving to the upper side of Shouldville.

On the upper side of town live the "Should Masters." These are the elite; they pass in polite society based solely on their ability to mask their should-fest invitations in the guise of positivity.

A Should Master can mask their opening salvo so it sounds like a question or even praise.

Eventually I realized that even a Should Master still lived in Shouldville, and Shouldville is a dark, dank place where lives get lived and dreams go to die. I wanted out and discovered a way!

The way to move out of Shouldville is to STOP participating in or inviting should-fests! In other words, stop "shoulding" on yourself and others!

The fastest way to stop "shoulding" is to read the following, out loud and often . . .

Every penny I have ever spent was well spent – even if I would not choose to spend a penny that way today.

This is how you live a life of – no guilt.

Every second I have ever lived was well lived – even if I would not choose to live a second that way today.

This is how you live a life of – no regrets.

Every word I have ever read, every word a teacher ever said, was useful – even if I disagree with it.

This is how you live a life of – no judgement.

Every person I have ever met enriched my life in some way – even if I would not choose to spend a second with them today.

This is how you live a life of – no blame.

If you truly want to leave Shouldville and live a life of no guilt, regret, judgement, or blame, and spend more time in your Happy Place, simply follow the directions above, repeat often, and stay away from Shouldees!

To make the path out of Shouldville even faster visit:

www.EmotionalTeflon.com
for a free mindset-reset tool

13

Let Time Do Its Job

by Iman Aghay

A few years back, after my cancer was removed in 2012, I was really physically tired and ill. It was about 50 days after my surgery, and I needed to do something social.

And I wanted to get strong, so I decided to go on a climb on a hill because they said it was easy.

The climb was a way for me to know that I was healed and strong. My fellow hikers provided camaraderie and support as we set out. The social interaction bound us together as we were all ascending the hill at our own paces. Some walked quickly. Others walked leisurely.

I moved along well behind the crowd.

The hill had a gentle slope which gave it its hiking rank of "easy." About halfway up the hill I kind of blacked out and had to separate from the group. I couldn't even do an "easy" climb.

Well, today, 7 years later, I dropped off my car for a tire change and I actually found myself at the base of the same hill.

So, I decided to climb it and I realized that it's actually a very steep climb, even though they had rated it as easy.

I'm really very happy because I've realized that at times in life it feels like it kicks you down and it feels like there is no hope and there's no future – yet there is, there definitely is.

It just takes time; you just need to let time do its job.

And then you'll be able to get to something that felt once like a huge, massive goal. In fact, you'll be able to do it on a regular basis with regular shoes, not even walking shoes.

If you let time do its job, you'll eventually find yourself on the top of your hill.

14

Lust For Life
by Rebeca Forero

I am 47 years old, married to a wonderful man, mother of four stunning children, and grandmother of two beauties. Having this happy little gang is my biggest achievement. We went through many obstacles on our way to happiness.

Tough experiences have shaped me in different areas, too. My childhood wasn't easy. My parents divorced when I was two years old and I just remember having a mother that mentally abused me; a father that physically abused me; a stepfather that sexually abused me; three younger brothers that I had to take care of, but also a stepmother that was my support . . . my angel.

Every time that I got hit by my dad, every time that I shared with my stepmom the stupid things my mom said, she was always there to give me hope and love. She always said that "one day, everything was going be OK." Of course, she didn't know about the sexual abuse, but when I was living that experience, I always remembered her words.

I truly believe that, depending on our decisions, we can change our realities either to make them better or to make them worse. I chose to believe that "one day, everything was going be ok," and decided to fight for it. My traumatic experiences have given me the strength and will to stand in defense of other victims; to become a natural advocate for the well-being of others. I have fought for justice for sexual assault victims in the role of advocate. My tragedy has brought me understanding of the pain and suffering of other victims.

I can't change my past; however, I actively influence my future in various fields. I am a challenge addict.

Understanding the perspective of other people, learning from their and my experiences, is another passion of mine.

I spend my days diving into the work that brings me joy. I work as an operations manager, Spanish interpreter, and staff leader at The Intraespa Intercultural Learning Center. I have a company that organizes corporate events. I'm a certified life coach and I'm passionate about fitness and health. Endorphins have a party inside of my body every time I dance, exercise, read, and learn about fashion or travel.

It is my life goal to inspire, help, guide, and support others. My weapons are my experiences, my voice, my failings, and my achievements.

15

Make A Stranger Smile, Today
by Ken Streater

My friend and fellow cofounder of "gud vyb," Mitch Rost, and I were on a flight home to Redmond, Oregon, after a business meeting in Southern California . . . Mitch and I spend a lot of time together coaching our daughters' sports teams, working out, and talking about community.

He's a physical therapist by trade, an inventor by avocation, and a philanthropist by nature. We often contemplate how to spread kindness but spend much more time laughing at and with other.

"gud vyb" (pronounced good vibe) is a result of those conversations and laughter. We created the gud vyb app in order to proliferate and amplify giving to one another, while at the same time contributing to vital charities. Actually, he invented the app; I am riding in the tailwind of his genius.

This particular flight home from Southern California happened before we had firmly landed on the gud vyb concept, but the conversation we had on that flight was integral to the project. We were deep in conversation about making the world better – or maybe just discussing the texture of our shoelaces – when we decided to create a list of ways people could make each other feel better or at least make someone else smile.

At the top of the list of how to share good vibes was simply to smile at someone in hopes that they would smile back. We have all done this, given a quick smile and a nod to someone who gives you a polite response in kind. However, research indicates that receiving a genuine smile can improve happiness and increase faith in others, while quick, insincere grins can engender a lack of trust.

With this data in mind, we concluded that if brief smiles did not guarantee a positive heart-felt response, then maybe something that took more time might.

After debating the amount of time it would take to inspire a genuine smile in another person, we decided to experiment. Our back-of-the-napkin reasoning led us to believe that if you could smile non-stop at nothing in particular for 20 seconds that you would: (1) look like a weirdo, (2) make the person who was watching you smile, or (3) both.

So, we tried it on each other. I had an aisle seat on the plane and Mitch was sitting by the window. The middle seat was unoccupied, which to this day we regard as a blessing for whoever would have been there.

After four rounds of rock-paper-scissors to determine who went first, I sat with a smile on my face, looking around and at Mitch for around 12 seconds. He quickly broke and cracked up. Then he went. About nine seconds into his happy-go-lucky grin, I smiled from ear to ear.

We decided to experiment more widely with our 20-seconds theory. Our plane landed in Seattle, and we headed to the food court during our layover.

After burritos – and several minutes into our test – we were likely regarded by our hungry fellow travelers as two very strange dudes or recent lottery winners. I would smile off into space for 20 seconds while Mitch scanned the crowd to see if anyone smiled at my smiling.

A couple of people did, but most looked away, hoping not to make eye contact with the bizarre (activity) before them. Then Mitch would go. Same response.

It was fun just smiling away, but we realized that this tactic was not the best way to get a stranger to smile or make someone feel better. We did, however, find quantifiable and repeatedly verifiable evidence that people eating at the next table would find another place to sit.

People mentally more stable probably would have packed it in at this point. But we didn't. Instead, we came up with better ideas, which we created into a simple list of how to inspire strangers to smile and how to bring more joy to people's lives. We encourage you to try one or all of them or to create your own list. We also encourage you to take the next minute to smile for 20 seconds.

1. Pay for the coffee of the person behind you in line.

2. Buy a flower in the grocery store and give it to the checker.

3. Leave change in a vending machine.

4. Let the person behind you at the grocery store go in front of you regardless of how much is in his or her cart or basket.

5. Send your spouse, partner, or a friend flowers at work for no reason.

6. Write out your favorite positive quote and give it to someone who would find it meaningful.

7. Give someone a small packet of herb seeds that they can plant, even in a window box.

8. Write a friend a note of admiration and appreciation and put it under his or her windshield wiper.

9. Send dessert to a table of strangers.

10. Give someone a check for five dollars with the request that they fill in the blank "pay to the order of" line with their favorite charity and mail it in.

11. Make or buy two lunches and give one away.

12. Compliment someone in front of others.

13. Tell your favorite joke to someone at work.

14. Give a kid a fist bump or high five.

15. Add a candy bar to your groceries at the checkout stand and give it to the person behind you as you finish checking out.

16. Give a friend a box of herbal tea.

17. Order pizza to be randomly delivered to your co-workers.

18. Say "way to go" to someone running by on a trail or at the gym.

19. Notice something good about the next person you see and say so to him or her.

20. Dance to no music in front of a group of people. (OK, never mind. Mitch and I will handle this one.)

(excerpt from: *Be The Good: Becoming A Force For A Better World*)

16

Manual For Misfits

by Kate Frank

I can't tell you the number of people who have told me to not write about this topic using the term 'misfits.' Most people find the word offensive or denigrating. I find being called a misfit a compliment.

So, what does it mean to be a misfit?

- It means you don't fit in.
- It means you are not average.
- It means you stand out from the crowd.

I don't know about you, but those things sound awesome to me. Look around at the adults you admire. Are they average? Of course, they aren't.

Misfits have a unique opportunity to leverage their unusual characteristics to become something outstanding. Those who embrace the part of them perceived as mis-fitting and move through life with the confidence of their great gifts . . . those are the people who change the world.

Welcome to My World if You Are a Misfit

I have always been a misfit, by any definition. I suppose the reason why I was able to embrace my misfit status early in life was because I was a pretty sickly child. Yet I was precocious, tenacious, and persistent.

As a young child, I had to deal with multiple trips to the hospital where my mother was told I would die. I always had some kind of ugly rash on my skin. My Sunday School teacher explained to my class I would have been sent to a leprosy colony if I were born in biblical times. My own dermatologist, who once had me hooked on drugs (a cocktail of steroids and tranquilizers), got angry and said, "When are you going to accept the fact you will never be normal?"

Misfits Change the World Every. Single. Day.

Why would I ever want to be normal if it meant I would be as unkind as my teacher or doctor? Who would want to be like them? You want to be better, don't you?

With this kind of exposure to normal vs misfit, I have always looked for people who don't fit in. You can find them everywhere and they are leading exceptional lives. Among the misfits you will find are people like Steve Jobs,

Leonardo DaVinci, Martin Luther King, recent Emmy Award winner Ali Stroker, Stephen Hawking, Michael J. Fox, Steven Spielberg, Whoopi Goldberg, Keira Knightley, Michael Phelps. The list could go on and on.

These are the people making a difference. The kid who is popular because they fit the normal expectations of their peers and teachers is not making a big impact on the world.

Embrace Your Weird

If anything, I have said so far makes sense to you, I am happy for you. Yet, you may not know how to take my outlook on being a misfit and integrate it into your daily life. Let me share some of the things I have done:

- Don't allow anyone to feel sorry for you. You don't need their sympathy.
- Accept the fact your weird bits are a gift from Your Maker.
- Be okay with having people around you who just don't get it.
- When people try to bully you into being normal, simply walk away, in confidence.
- Surround yourself with others who have their own weird bits.
- Don't limit yourself to people who are weird in the same way as you.

- When you can't quite understand another misfit person, particularly if they are different from you, be curious. Ask questions.

- If someone is having trouble coping with their own version of being out of the norm, offer your help any way you can.

- Ask your weird community to help you when you need it.

Remember Your Gift

You may have trouble remembering your weird, misfit nature is a gift. When this happens, I encourage you to use a tool to boost your confidence. First, identify what makes you a misfit or a weirdo. Then, use the phone you are holding in your hand to start a little research. Find successful people with similar misfit characteristics.

I don't care what your weirdness is, you will find someone. Let this success story be an anchor for your pride. Connect with their success on a deep and meaningful level. This person made it through feeling misfit and became a successful adult.

You can, too. Never forget it.

Never give up on yourself because you are a misfit. Instead, celebrate your own way of being in this world. You are here for a reason. Embrace your purpose and the world will show you how much they value who you are.

17

Move The Wall

by Linnea Appleby

When I was a child, my dad would say "Use your head" or "Think;" but mostly he would grab me by the shoulders, look deeply into my eyes, and say "Linnea, you can do anything you put your mind to."

Big words for a little girl. I grew up believing him, of course; he is my dad. We didn't have much money, but we never went without. I was lucky that my dad could fix stuff. He was always working on a car or boat to make extra cash and he tried to teach me whenever the opportunity arose. I'm pretty sure I learned my first curse words under a car.

We were instilled with a strong work ethic and learned the value of money early. One day there was a help wanted sign in the window of the local candy store. At first, my mother was horrified to learn I had interviewed for and gotten a job at 13 years old for 50 cents an hour selling penny candy and art supplies. Three years later, when I was 16, my parents bought the place. It needed a lot of work.

One weekend I watched as my dad and some of his buddies cut an entire wall from where it was, move it in one piece and reinstall it in another location. They just cut it, picked it up, and moved it. Now, I'm sure it wasn't that easy. They planned out what they were going to do and how they were going to do it, and everyone knew their role but then, easy-peasy it was done.

It may not seem like much, but it was an AHA moment for me. In an instant I understood how things that look impossible are not. I learned that if you don't like where the wall is, you can just move it. I saw that it took a team effort and understood the value of the right people in your life. For me that day shaped the direction of my life.

It did not mean that suddenly everything was easy, but it proved that if I thought and used my head, I could do anything I put my mind to. With that mindset, I started to say "Yes," or "let's try" to things that might have appeared a little more difficult or impossible to others. I would think about how I could overcome the obstacles to reach the goal. I recognized that successful people carried the same attitude. They were not afraid to try, not afraid to fail, and most importantly, not afraid to succeed.

I started to seek out and learn from the people who were leading the type of successful life I wanted. Not just money but a meaningful life that included abundance, strong friendships, respect, independence, and happiness. I read books, attended seminars, and talked with people I thought I could learn from by listening for the nuggets of wisdom that could help me shape my life into what I wanted it to be rather than letting life happen to me. I learned it was OK and even necessary to distance myself from people or things that did not fit into the life I was creating.

Once I learned about the "Law of Attraction," and other important messages from books like The Secret, The Power of Now, Mutant Message Down Under, and any book written by Malcom Gladwell, I incorporated affirmations and a powerful attitude of gratitude into my life.

It's never too late or too early to change the direction of your life.

You are always only one decision from a completely different life. If you don't like where the wall is, move it. Hang out with people who will help you move the wall, not those that tell you that you can't. Be thankful for what you have right now. Focus your thoughts on the good in your life and you will get more of it. Think; use your head, and you can do anything you put your mind to.

18

Night Sky

by Nadine Vernon

It all started in elementary school: the stares, the whispers, the giggling as he passed by. A deep sadness filled his being as his tormentors became more and more open. He no longer participated in class unless called upon. He began to withdraw at recess, often standing alone or going off to read under the shade of a tree. No one ever chose him to be on a team. No one ever asked him to play tag or kickball. He was labeled "strange" by his peers.

Middle school gave him more places to seek solitude, but the sadness never went away. Walking in the halls was a daily torment. Students purposefully bumped into him and called him names. After school he immersed himself in hobbies: drawing, story writing, and listening to music. He preferred staying in his room: this continued until he reached high school.

The first month of high school a new student transferred in from out of state. She, too, was a loner, but her solitude was self-imposed. She had little regard for her fellow classmates and clearly was not impressed with them. As chance would have it, she saw him sitting alone behind the stacks in a study carrel in the library and decided to sit next to him.

Paying no attention to the shushing librarian, she peppered him with questions. He was so startled when he answered them all. She matter-of-factly stated that they should be friends and abruptly got up, leaving him sitting wondering if she was pulling a prank.

As the days ensued, he learned more and more about her: how she hated posers, hated cliques, and wanted to escape to an island of free thinkers. He had no idea where this island was located on the globe, but she was self-assured and said that she had a plan.

Their friendship grew as the school year progressed. He slowly began to share his written stories and drawings with her. She admired the way in which he expressed himself on paper and applauded his creations. She soothed his sadness and he felt understood. Her acceptance created a bond that no other person had offered to him. The daily tormenting of his peers had not ceased, but he was able to withstand the onslaught of comments because he knew that she was a kindred spirit. Together they forged an alliance to which no one else was privy.

One day in the Spring she arrived at school appearing quite animated and asked him to play hooky from their afternoon classes. He was tempted to join her on the adventure, but he felt an uneasiness in her demeanor and decided to remain in school. She flashed him a smile and proceeded to leave by a side exit that the custodial staff normally used. Running, hoping to not be seen, she entered the state park that bordered the school grounds. Trails crisscrossed the entire forest and she hiked disappearing from sight.

The next morning as students sat in homerooms an announcement came over the intercom. His friend, surrounded by nature's beauty, had taken her own life. Why had she done this? Outwardly she appeared unabashed and confident. He, by contrast, was introverted and fearful. She had not been bullied so it just did not make sense to him. Questions only led to more questions with no satisfactory answers.

He challenged himself to find a way in which to have good come from his deep heartache.

That month after her death he formulated a plan to create a support group program for teens within the high school. Overcoming his fears, he approached administrators, guidance counselors, faculty members, the school nurse, and the PTA. By becoming an advocate for struggling peers, he raised his self-esteem. Adults helped him research formats to address stress, loneliness, bullying, and other at-risk factors. He presented his idea at a district board meeting and the plan was approved.

Interact, Key Club, DECA, FBLA, NHS and Red Cross clubs all adopted the support group as a service project. He began speaking at Rotary and Kiwanis meetings to raise awareness about bullying and teen suicide, presenting his mission to have these groups within schools throughout his city, state, nation and around the world. Through the loss of his friend and his own heartache, a call-to-action had emerged to help others in similar circumstances.

By focusing on a positive act, negativity moved to the background and healing could take place.

One action and one voice can change your own life and that of others.

"When it is darkest, we can see the stars."
– *Ralph Waldo Emerson*

19

No Money. No Credit.
No College?

by Denise Thomas

"But Mom! How am I going to go to college?"

Mom, just shook her head, put aside her coffee and said, "Let's talk . . ."

I was just starting high school. The last few years had been rough. Dad was laid off twice from his job and used retirement funds to try to keep the house. We went bankrupt and lost the house anyway, along with everything else.

I still remember strangers coming into the house and buying everything we had. Every book, every game, pots and pans, furniture, even our dogs had to go. That was probably the hardest part. I had a sinking feeling of not knowing what was next. Where would we go? Where would we live? Why did "my stuff" have to go? There was only enough money left to buy a trailer and a lawn mower so dad could start mowing lawns.

We moved to a small 2-bedroom apartment. I expected to share a room with my little brother, but the apartment was too small to put two beds in one room, so my brother slept on the couch. We moved several times trying to make ends meet. Then the truck got repossessed. Luckily a friend gave us an old one to use for the business. That was a Godsend!

Eventually, Dad was able to hire one man, then two men. It became a real business. He said, showing up when you said you would was a large part of the success. He was right. Of course, he learned what it takes to do a really good job. You'd be surprised what you can learn on YouTube. But to him, it was about integrity. Just do what you said. He built the business on that.

I was 13 when we lost it all. That next year, starting high school, my mom realized affording college seemed impossible. She knew we didn't have the money to pay for it. And with a bankruptcy, they couldn't co-sign for a loan. There had to be a way. Mom began to do the research.

She learned about scholarships and read about different colleges and what their expectations were. Mom explained that there was only so much she could do to help me get into college or to pay for it. The work, she said, would be up to me. I had to do my best in school. I had to participate in activities that I found interesting. And I would have to write essays for college scholarship contests.

Dad got a job back in the corporate world a few years before I graduated high school. That made paying the bills easier, but there was still no money for college. Having a "normal" job meant he now made too much for financial aid.

To make matters worse, I wasn't your typical high school student. I was homeschooled. I had no "college coach" and no high school counselor, so my mom was my high school counselor. Mom found a few organizations for high school students that gave scholarships to their members; but being homeschooled, I was not allowed to join.

Filling out applications for scholarships drove home just how different being homeschooled made me. My applications had "gaps" – great big gaping holes. Where "normal" kids checked boxes of their high school clubs and activities, I had nothing. I thought I was special. But special meant I wasn't like everyone else. It seemed the deck was stacked against me.

Things began to turn in my favor. The summer before junior year I took practice ACT tests using old prep books I found at used bookstores. I took the ACT exam several times that year. My best test score was in December. It was good enough to guarantee the lowest level of scholarship at many colleges. But it wasn't enough.

I applied for outside scholarships that year. The money comes, not from the college, but from organizations or businesses. I'm sure I wrote at least one essay every weekend. Did it get tiring? Absolutely. And although some of the scholarships were for as little as $300, it was more than I had in the bank yesterday. I ended up winning several scholarships from $500 to $10,000 just writing essays.

By the time I began my freshmen year at a state university I had my first year paid for and much of the remaining years as well. I worked during school, and continued applying for scholarships, adding two more. In the end, I graduated college with $2000 left over.

Many will say you have to either have money or take out loans to go to college. We had no money. And I didn't have to take out loans. What I did have was an absolute determination to go to college and do it debt free. Never put all your eggs in one financial basket. Work, and work some more. Do your best in school and do what you love.

This is my daughter's story. She went to college debt free and so did my son. Where there is a will, there is a way. There is always hope. Don't let anyone tell you you can't do it. Prove them wrong.

20

No More Programs

by Joy Resor

Life has taught me that changing ONE thing can change EVERYTHING!

Like those who give up smoking or start daily walking.

Like the friend who stopped eating ice cream every night after dinner.

Like the day I moved after divorce into an unfurnished home.

I'd decided that this would be a good time to experiment... to try NOT having a television set after decades as a program-addicted person.

As a child, I loved watching shows including Gilligan's Island, The Monkees, and Let's Make a Deal.

As a working woman, I joined the lunchroom gang watching Days of Our Lives, with Jeopardy and Fame after dinner.

As a stay-at-home mom my favorites were Oprah and Dr. Phil, with family shows at night. And . . . of course . . . sports.

In a household where I was the lone female, baseball games, football games, and golf tournaments were prime programming.

Until . . . I was a single woman moving into an unfurnished home, since I'd left TVs behind when I moved from the home my husband and I had shared.

Can you see that first evening without television? Oh, my. How am I going to live without watching American Idol? How am I going to spend evenings without television?

I called a new neighbor I'd met to ask if she watches American Idol. No, I don't.

Yikes!

Hmm . . . my addiction can't be fed tonight.

Breathe, Joy . . . breathe.

So be it.

I don't recall exactly what I did, but I imagine that I wrote in my journal and picked up a book or took a long bath.

I do recall that as the days unfolded, days lasted much longer than EVER, and I accomplished more than I EVER thought I could.

Time expanded!

Without television, I had time to take walks, to connect with friends, and to create a gratitude and spiritual practice.

Without programs, I started a journey to bring love, peace, and joy to the world.

When YOU change one little thing, how will EVERYTHING change for YOU?

Go for it!

Enjoy yourself!

Let me know!

21

The Skeen Machine

by Ilene Skeen

In the early '90s, I received a big promotion to manage a group of 25 people. Those 25 people's work supported about 400 clerks, analysts, and managers in six different departments of the company. My group had so many jobs, tasks, and deadlines that they were running in circles. I just wanted to throw up my hands and quit. I must have sounded desperate when I vented my complaint to my teenage son, who said, *"Mom, you have it all backwards. It doesn't matter how many jobs you have piled up on your plate. The only jobs that matter are the jobs you can do."*

"First, you have Job 1. Job 1 is the job you can do. It's the job that you know how to do and can accomplish. It's all set up. It's waiting for you to do it. You're ready to do it. You do it. You're done! Finished! Put it on your list of accomplishments.

"Then Job 2 comes along. Job 2 is the job you think about. You figure out what steps you need to do the job. You set up the job

so that you can do it, but you don't do it. You leave it. **You don't do it."**

"The next job is Job 3.... "

When my son finished his lecture a minute later, I had only a one-word, "Wow!" I knew he was right.

I told my group. We turned the many projects into a process. It was like a machine. The result was astounding. The backlog cleared. My team was happy and so were our users. An analyst christened it the "Skeen Machine." Unstoppable.

The Skeen Machine can control the flow of any work. I use it to direct my thought processes to be most effective. I can even guide my subconscious thought processes. The Skeen Machine also helps me manage my emotions, fears, and expectations.

Any teen desiring to grow into an empowered adult can use the Skeen Machine and make it their own.

22

Start As Soon as You Wake Up

by Joyce Blue

Whether you are going to have a great day or not is a decision you get to make every day. It really is that easy. I know we all face tons of junk in our lives, and I didn't used to believe any of this when I was younger. You CAN have a great day every day, so start as soon as you wake up.

Every morning upon waking, yawn and stretch. It helps circulate the fluids in your body that have pooled while you slept.

Think of at least one thing (and if you can think of three, that's even better) you are grateful for before you get out of bed. You can also write it in a gratitude journal you keep by your bed. Then you can re-read it on tough days when you need some inspiration. As you practice gratitude in your life, you'll find more things to be grateful for. It's a very powerful practice.

Throughout the day, stay focused on the positive outcomes you want. If you have a test you're afraid to take, prepare ahead of time and envision getting the paper back with an "A" on it. The grade won't just happen, you'll have to do your part and prepare for the test. If you focus on the bad or scary things, your day and your outcomes won't be as good as if you stay focused on the positive outcomes you want.

Give service to others, even if it's just a smile, warm hello, or holding the door for someone. Giving service to others helps you take your mind off your own life and is a blessing to those you are serving. You can change someone else's entire day with a kind, sincere smile.

Be aware when you start feeling angry. Pause, take a deep breath, and count to 10 before responding. Once I started doing this in my own life it was amazing what a huge difference it made. You can even write a note or email to get your frustrations out. Just don't address it to the person, or for email don't put in the email address. The intent isn't to send it. It's to let you vent to get your frustrations out on something the words won't harm. Then rip up the paper or delete the email.

I learned a great acronym: H.A.L.T., which stands for Hungry, Angry, Lonely, & Tired. Never make big decisions, send text messages or email, or do anything out of spite (ever). It's especially important when you're hungry, angry, lonely, or tired.

Remember life always works out if you do your part to do what's right, even when it seems like it's crashing in on you. Sometimes things have to "fall apart" in order for them to fall into place for your greatest good. I have a client who wanted a job so badly but was turned down multiple times. She finally met someone who worked there, and they put in a good word for her. She eventually got hired and quit her other job. It was only a few months before she was totally miserable. She realized the job wasn't anything like she thought it was going to be, and she was super sorry she had "wasted" a year trying to get hired at this company.

There is no such thing as failure. In life you win, you learn, or both. Failure can be one of four blessings:

The 1st blessing is learning. Each time something doesn't go right in your life you can always learn something from that experience.

The 2nd blessing is being redirected. Maybe you are being redirected from one relationship to another, or one job to another. Often you don't see this until you have some space between yourself and the experience.

The 3rd blessing is reflection. Each time you "fail," it's good to take a step back and see what you could have done differently or better, so that next time you can handle things differently. It gives you a chance to go inward and reflect.

The 4th blessing is the set up. Catastrophic events in your life set you up for bigger and better things. Later you can look back and see how you were being guided to something better.

Challenges are a part of life.
It's all in how you respond to them.
So, start making it a great day as soon as you wake up.

23

The Successful Path of Failure
by Danielle Silverman, MBA, M.A., ACC

When I was 15 years old, I told my dad I wanted to become a doctor. I don't know what I expected in telling him. Maybe I thought he would be proud of me . . . Maybe I thought he would encourage me . . . Maybe I thought he might have some advice for me . . . After all, there were other doctors in the family. It didn't seem like a big stretch.

Here's what he said to me:

"I know you. I know you as well as I know what's in my pocket. As a matter of fact, I wish I knew what was in my pocket as well as I know you. You'll never be a doctor."

I didn't react right away. I was very much an introvert, and I didn't reply. I didn't know how to reply. I went back to doing whatever it was I was doing. Over time, in a most unconscious way, I proceeded to try to prove him wrong.

After grade 10, I moved to another school that I thought had a much higher science curriculum. I excelled there, taking extra biology classes, getting straight As. At the age of 19, without having been to any college or university, I applied to medical school. At first, I was put on a waiting list, and then a space opened, and I got in. I couldn't believe it!

My first year of medical school was grueling. Dissecting a cadaver was WAY different from dissecting a fetal pig. Now, for the first time in my life, I was confronted with death in a very, very real way. Not only seeing a dead human body, but living through the illness and eventual death of my beloved uncle at the same time, was distressing.

I had also experienced death when I was only three years old and had never come to terms with that. So, staring death in the face at 19 was reliving the trauma of the 3-year-old.

Not surprisingly, I failed that first year of medical school. I left, licking my wounds. Had my dad been right after all?

After spending the next few months working in a mindless job, I decided to go back to school and get a university undergraduate degree, but I still hadn't learned what I needed to learn. I enrolled in a curriculum of Life Sciences, which meant I was again studying anatomy, physiology, and biochemistry – just not working on a human cadaver.

Of all the courses I was taking, I had the most trouble with biochemistry. I didn't understand it. None of it made sense. I couldn't remember any of it because there wasn't any logic that I could figure out. By Christmas of my last year, I was failing all my courses.

I didn't understand how I could have gone from loving a subject so much to failing at it so miserably. I decided to go and see a school counselor.

He listened to my story and said: "There is nothing to understand about biochemistry. You just need to memorize it. Oh (by the way) you're simply in the wrong field for you."

Wow! I was blown away. You mean all I need to do is learn by heart? I can do that. Beyond that, it felt like such a relief to hear from someone else that it was OK to realize that this was not the right field of study for me.

For the rest of year, I worked my butt off to make sure I got at least 80% in all my final exams, just so I could pass all my courses and leave that university with a degree, even if my GPA was low.

At least I had a degree. I could figure out the rest of it later. I'm not a quitter. I see things through to the end. I learned that about myself that year.

The only problem that was left was that I didn't know what I was meant to do. I never thought of asking the school counselor how I could figure it out. Today, I also know that it was probably partly his responsibility to ask me if I wanted to find out and suggest a path on how to get there. Sadly, that didn't happen.

That was more than 40 years ago. It's been a circuitous road to find my path. I've learned that it takes some people longer than others. It's OK. Trust your gut. Try out different things. Ask for help. It takes longer and is more difficult when you try to do it alone.

A mentor of mine once said: "We are not what we do or what we choose to do, but who we become while we're doing whatever it is we do."

There's only one very special you.
Be yourself.
Enjoy the journey.

24

Ten Words of Wisdom I Wish I Had As A Teen

by Jessica Peterson

Ahh . . . to be young again! I recall being a teenager and thinking how much I wished to be an adult. As an adult I could get away from the mess at home and have a life I desired and wanted.

I remember in high school being told that there was a special program for five kids who had the worst life. My sister and I were selected to be a part of it. A counselor would come in and we would talk out our problems. At the time I remember thinking, "Why are we talking about our problems? Should we not be talking about solutions or a positive and hopeful future?"

Fast forward: I immersed myself into my career. Throughout that time, I worked a lot on personal development. Today I'm a real estate agent, business coach, life coach, best-selling author, speaker, wife, mom, and more! What I accomplished is above my wildest dreams. If I can do it, you can too!

There are many things I discovered along the way and what I discovered was money is not everything. I started wondering "if there is a God, why is there suffering?" You can now google that subject and find some great information. Here is some information I wish I knew when I was a teenager:

1. Relationships are important and so are mentors. I wish I had mentors as a teenager. If there is someone you look up to, reach out to them! Good news for teenagers today: there is the internet. Be selective who you follow and look up to. You do become like the people you associate with. It never hurts to reach out and ask someone if they would be willing to mentor you. If someone says no, just remember the right mentor is right around the corner! It is important to get together on the phone or meet in person with people. Relationships solely from the internet or social media are not rewarding. People will come and go in your life. There is only so much room for the right people. When someone leaves your life, that is ok! It leaves room for the right people. Quality people over quantity is much more fulfilling in life. Who can you reach out to today?

2. Personal development is important. The more you invest in you, the "richer" you will be. What book or online resource can you read today to be a better you?

3. Remember that thoughts are powerful. You become what you think about. Changing what you think about can be easier said than done. Visualize daily first thing in the morning what your day will look like. What would you like the rest of your day to be like?

4. Write out all your dreams and go after them! Realize that sometimes the steps to be taken to make it happen are right in front of you. Other times they are not so obvious. The more you think about it and visualize it happening, at the right time an answer will come and give you solutions! What can you write today?

5. Listening is vital. There is so much to learn. Be selective about who and what you listen to. Your mind grows and expands based on what it is fed. What do you listen to daily?

6. Be careful not to trust all people right away. There are good and bad people. Focus on finding the good ones. Who do you wish to know better?

7. Show love and kindness. The world deserves more of it! And don't forget to be loving and kind to YOU!

You deserve the best! What can you do today to take care of you?

8. Balance is essential. I write about it in my book, Create a WOW Life. Life is like driving a car. When you get a flat tire, you don't go very far. The tires represent four key areas to balance. They are wealth, health, relationships, and faith/social impact. What is one goal in each area on which you can improve? I want to see you drive and go after your dreams. You need all four tires full and happy!

9. Reflect on these tips and look for ways to improve. We can all improve in life.

10. The final word of wisdom is to celebrate! So often we forget to celebrate the beautiful gift of life. You can celebrate small and big wins. How can you celebrate today?

25

Those Darker Years
by Mary Schrank

My first two years in college led me down a path that was about as far from how I was raised as it could have been.

I don't talk about this much, not because I'm trying to create a perfect image of myself; but to be honest, I simply forget about those challenging times as the abundance of God's blessings overshadow them. I know I've been forgiven, and I know without a doubt they have made me a better person for having lived through them.

I didn't dress the same, I didn't speak the same, I didn't act the same; there were drugs, there was alcohol, there was an extra 30 pounds, there were too many boys, there were stories that I probably shouldn't be alive to even retell, there were FAR TOO MANY bad choices . . . but there was always one constant, beautiful, blessing that NEVER, EVER, EVER, left me ~ The Holy Spirit!

He had such a BIG GIGANTIC PLAN for my life that He protected me every second of every day during those years so that I could fulfill His plans for my life. I have been asked many times if I wished I could "erase" those darker years and my answer is always the same . . . ABSOLUTELY NOT! I have no doubt that my drive to help others "operate from their place of greatness" comes directly from those years. So, today I say, GOD SAVES ME! He saved me during those darker years and continues to save me every single day . . . using me as His vessel to help His people . . . allowing me to fulfill His BIG PLANS for my life!

Perhaps there are big plans for your life as well . . .

26

To Stay or To Go
by Katie Miller

When I was 16, I had a part-time job where I worked weekends. I liked my job and had fun at work most of the time. I also liked hanging out with my friends every Sunday evening at youth group. One Sunday, the youth pastor announced that he was planning a 3-day retreat for us. Over the following week, my friends and I talked non-stop about this retreat.

When I went to work and requested the time off, I was told no. There were other co-workers who had already requested off for that same weekend and the store would be shorthanded. I was torn. I liked my job and wanted to show I could be responsible and trustworthy for work, but I really wanted to go on the trip.

I decided to talk this out with friends, parents, the youth pastor, and compare notes between them. The answer became clear that it was my decision to make. After going back and forth, weighing what to do, I decided I was going to go on the retreat. Regardless of the consequences, I knew it was the right thing for me to do for my spiritual wellbeing.

Now, the hard part was telling the boss. I decided to go into work after school the next day to discuss the issue. When I spoke with my boss, I explained how important this retreat was to me. I explained that although I knew that I did not have the time off approved, I would not be coming into work that weekend. I acknowledged that I might not have a job when I returned, but I hoped that I did when I got back.

That was one of the hardest decisions I made as a teenager. I put my job in jeopardy for a retreat with my youth group.

While on the retreat, I learned a great deal about myself. We created journals to keep track of what we learned and accomplished over the course of the retreat. There were several group and individual activities to build trust in ourselves and others. I came home recharged and more confident that I had made the right choice.

The next day, I stopped by work after school to check the schedule. What relief I felt when I saw my name on the schedule. I got to keep my job and I was not being "punished" for standing up for myself.

Thinking back now, I can see how this affected another choice concerning my career. I had several jobs where I was not happy and dreaded to go into work, but I needed a paycheck to support my family.

One day, while talking to my mom, I was complaining about my latest job. My mom suggested I try something new. I knew I was unhappy with my job, but I needed to take care of my family.

On a leap of faith, I applied for a corporate job. When I was called in for an interview, I decided I would be myself and be honest with what I wanted in a job. The very next week, I received a call. They were offering me the job with the requests I had made.

Now, I can support my family doing a job that I love. Looking back, having the courage to do what I felt was right for me as a teenager helped provide the courage needed to pursue new opportunities as an adult.

27
U B U
by Kris Bell

Wondering where you fit in?

Think that you don't?

Awesome!

You are our problem solvers, our forward thinkers, our "Something's gotta change, and I'm the one to do it!" people. Dare to be you.

Some of us just don't fit in a box . . .

Wha Hoo!! Thank goodness. How absolutely refreshing. Keep being you!

We need you, the "dancers to your own drums," the originals, the "Authentics!"

The one who isn't understood, the Wild Child.

Own it, it's yours.

You are enough, as you are.

You are magnificent.

Be so proud of your uniqueness, your style, and your own way of seeing and of Be-ing.

Someone is always admiring you.

Wishing they could be as free spirited as you. To express themselves like you.

It may come out sideways at times, but the reality is they admire you. Even if you can't see it right now.

Someone is always impressed with you.

Take the time to find out what truly makes you tick.

What makes your soul sing, dance, come alive? Then choose that for YOURself.

I see you.

You are magnificent.

You are all that you need.

Shine your beautiful light so the rest of us can see what Awesome really is.

28

What Makes It A Great Day?

by Mike Jones

As I have been thinking about this task for several days, it has brought about many ideas of things I do. I have come to a deeper realization about which things are most effective and I am more cognizant of doing more each day to make it a great day.

People, for the most part, experience many of the same circumstances each day. How you handle these circumstances or challenges defines your character and determines your future.

Every day, I wake up thankful to be alive. I appreciate all I have. I appreciate my health, family, friends, and all the things in my past that have made me what I am today. The struggles and challenges have made me stronger, wiser, and more grateful for the things I have.

When presented with a situation during the day, I choose to be positive. I look for the good and think to myself, *many people have far worse situations.* For example, if the electricity goes out and I'm late for work, I think, somewhere there is a homeless person that would love to have electricity, a home, and a job.

I use self-talk continuously throughout the day to keep my mind in a positive state and get through challenges.

They help me a lot to make it a great day. "Make the next right choice," "one hour (minute, second, class, etc.) at a time" . . . "things will get better," "keep it simple," "easy does it," "it is what it is," "deal with it," "let go and let God." Those are but a few.

Other things I do to make it a great day is helping people. I hold doors. I help carry things. I compliment people. Always! I adjust my schedule to accommodate people. I listen when people talk. I take on more responsibility if someone is struggling. I put myself in other people's shoes, look at things from a different perspective.

I am patient with people. I set goals for myself, daily goals to accomplish two or three things that need to be done to take care of myself mentally and physically. I picture myself achieving those goals. I breathe and take a step back if I feel my red flags going up (signs that I'm not being positive).

Most importantly, I reflect on my day. Every day! What could I have done better? What can I do tomorrow to help me reach my goals? Do I need to apologize for any of my actions? Did I surround myself with positive people? Did I stay away from drama and negative people?

I also read. Where I work, our principal is helping the staff keep a positive mindset. He has bought us many books which teach us how to stay positive and how to teach the students to be positive and never give up.

And finally, I give myself a break once in a while. I am my own worst critic. I can beat myself up mentally better than anyone I know. I have to remind myself that I'm human and I make mistakes and it's ok. I have to be kind to myself.

Making it a great day is a work in progress, and requires effort, and I continue to learn more every day.

29

What's On Your Shirt?

by Erin Strayer

It was a cool, rainy night – the best kind to sleep! I didn't want to wake up! I was all snuggled in, comfy, but my eye was bothering me. My left eye to be exact. I tried rubbing it as everyone does. That only made it worse. Geesh, do I really have to get out of bed to figure this eye thing out?

Stumbling to the bathroom at barely 12 minutes after six am on the first day of summer break, was this how it was going to be? I should still be sleeping and enjoying waking up on my own on. But it seemed that this was how my life has been lately. Nothing seemed to be going "my way" at all lately. Nothing!

Blinding myself with the bathroom light, my eye immediately got worse. What in the world happened overnight? Did I scratch my cornea while I was sleeping? I couldn't, could I? I wear a sleep mask to block out the pin-sized light on my wall switch. But did I move the mask?

Or did something get in there and was now irritating my eye like crazy? Had a bug crawled in my sleep mask? Or did I pick up some bacteria or virus from someone and now I had an infection? What in the world?!?!? I don't have time for this – UGH!

Attempting to pry my eyeball open to assess the situation, my brain power was slowly coming to, and the fog from sleep was lifting. All I can see is hot pink. How many nights had I slept in this pink t-shirt? Shaking my head, I tried to focus on my left eye situation. I did the usual evaluation of initial observation. It didn't look like it was scratched. It wasn't pink or irritated or discolored in any way.

Pulling the eye lid down, I didn't find any eyelashes floating around, that usually was the cause this type of painful situation and massive irritation. Rolling my eyes side to side, I noticed a shimmer in the inner corner. Did I really leave my contact in ALL NIGHT? What was going on?!? How could I take one out and not the other? They were "daily's" for God's sake, I wasn't supposed to even nap in them let alone sleep all night long!

After flushing my eye with the saline solution to wet that contact enough to release from its folded origami form in the corner of my eye, I was successful in getting it out. But why did I leave it in? Why would I take one out and not the other? I'm not forgetful! I'm not disorganized or distracted! I'm not too tired to forget something as simple as a stinkin' contact! WHAT am I not seeing here?!?

My eyes dropped to the hot pink t-shirt I was wearing, and I immediately wondered, again, how many nights I slept in this shirt? It's been one of my favorites as far as t-shirts go. I don't like t-shirts as a rule, on other people sure, but for me they are for sleeping or working in the yard. But this one . . . this one always made me smile and flash back quite a few years to when life was a bit different.

"Team Catching Hell" represented what I considered finally arriving! We were an elite fishing team made up of three semi-professional (amateur) females who joined forces a few times during salmon season to bring home trophies and cash, making our husbands proud, sharing a lot of laughs, and outranking others in the tight knit community of tournament anglers.

Our last season fishing together, and our biggest win got us these hot pink t-shirts, a 3-foot-tall shiny purple trophy, a lot of cash, a photo op, a magazine spread and a lot of bragging rights. We were seen as "holding our own" and the "ones to watch" from the competition and upheld our coveted name.

But this morning, as I was digging this contact out of my eye, I SAW my Team Catching Hell shirt . . . maybe for the first time it actually landed.

This t-shirt had its proud logo on the front left chest and my name all in caps on the right, and a full logo on the back . . . Team Catching Hell. What did this say about me? Does this shirt really represent me and my amazing teammates that are respected professionals and leaders in their positions? Does this shirt represent who I am NOW?

Tough questions at 6:30 am! Why do I still proudly take care of this shirt even though it's not who I am anymore nor what I stand for or represent? Kicking ass and taking names, stacking up trophies, cash and notoriety . . . that's not me . . . is it? Maybe it never was and only that I wanted it to be or the only way that I would ever get recognized or ahead . . . WHOA!

It got me wondering about the other t-shirts in my closet that I reserve for "casual" days. What did they say about me and who I am now? I had to go look at my stack of t-shirts because I was starting to hyperventilate. What was I saying to whoever reads my shirt(s) or for that matter what I was putting in my body's personal energy field? And what was the message I was telling myself?

I ran to my closet and started frantically pulling out one t-shirt after another: Camp Timbers, Boys and Girls Club, MSU, Cabo San Lucas, Kennedy Space Center, MFL Kids Fishing Tournament . . . then I got to the ones I was digging for. The ones that really represented ME! What I believe in and what I want to stand for daily! The ones I want people to remember and know ME by!

> "Breathe" - "Believe" - "Receive" - "I Am" - "Let's Reframe" - "Launch Leaders" - "Be the Solution"

These t-shirts absolutely represent exactly who and what I am today as a leader and expert trainer. Each one of these shirts has so many meanings and makes me think and re-evaluate who I am when I read them. Each one of these!

Ever since I can remember, I have been teaching people things. When I was eight, or maybe even younger, I taught the other little kids in the neighborhood how to properly catch and handle insects, bees, frogs, small animals, and snakes so not to hurt them, but learn about them.

I remember when I was 14, teaching kids at day camp where I was a counselor-in-training, how to make clay bowls out of dirt, clay, and grass; letting them sit in the sun to harden. When I got to college, I took pride in being a campus tour guide, tutor, and small group leader for incoming freshmen. As I continued with my medical career, I was always a leader; a teacher; a guide, and a mentor to others.

As life continued, I became a business co-owner at the age of 26 and experienced extremely fast company growth into multi-millions. I became a go-to resource for other companies and began speaking and telling our story.

I have always been a leader. Always concerned about what was on my shirt. Always representing.

Not always did I realize that was a leader nor was I being authentic or staying in my lane or even being in integrity.

Today, I got a huge slap in the face when my vision cleared from the forgotten contact lens. Today will be the last day I ever wear this hot pink Catching Hell t-shirt. It's not what I want to represent or have in my energy field.

So, what's on your shirt? Is it truly what you want to BE in this world and to represent? Do your t-shirts lead others to be inspired, positive, encouraged, happy, and full of joy? Think about it and then choose.

Today, I am choosing to change my energy and existence in the world by eliminating one potentially intimidating shirt that doesn't project or line up with my mission to inspire amazing humans to BE more.

What shirt will you choose?

About The Authors

It's All Inside of You
Becky Scheliga

Becky is a Success and Growth Mindset Coach. She spent most of her life struggling with extremely severe depression and anxiety. Later in her life she also developed and was diagnosed with PTSD. Her struggle to feel positive, confident, and worthy of really anything throughout her entire life was constant. After a suicide attempt and being on the verge of a second attempt, she came to look at life in a whole new way.

She decided that she wanted to make it her new mission in life to use all of her painful experiences as powerful lessons. She wanted to share all the things that she's been through and the lessons she learned to show that it is possible to change and it's never too late to become the person you want to be.

To learn more about Becky, visit:
https://www.linkedin.com/in/rebecca-scheliga-74b415186/

Getting to the Top of the Hill
Cody Dakota Wooten

 **Cody** is known as The Heroic Potential and Legendary Leadership Coach. His goal is to create the next generation of Legendary Leaders who will go out and drastically change the world for the better.

Cody's a sought-after speaker, the host of the Emerge Leadership Connection TV Show and Podcast, and the founder of The Leadership Guide, a LoCo Coyote Enterprises Company.

To learn more about Cody, visit: www.TheLeadership. Guide or www.EmergeLeadership.Club

The Successful Path of Failure
Danielle Silverman, MBA, M.A., ACC

 **Danielle** is an executive, leadership, change, and career coach. For the past 15 years, she has passionately helped individuals and organizations in transition. Danielle has a reputation for her warm and compassionate approach and for being able to draw people out and engage them in learning that will drive them forward in their careers and in their lives. She is a talented and versatile communicator and public speaker who brings to the table extensive expertise culled through more than 40 years of wide-ranging experience in management and marketing communication as well as business administration, project and event management, strategic planning, relationship management, career management and leadership and organizational development across numerous industries in both the private and public sectors.

As a coach, Danielle's mission is to work with people who want a change so they can do what they love - and be who they love - for the rest of their life.

To learn more about Danielle, visit:
www.DanielleSilverman.com

No Money. No Credit. No College?
Denise Thomas

Denise went from starving college student who "lifted" food from her college campus cafeteria to have meals for the weekend, to mom who figured out how to get colleges to beg her kids to attend their school. Denise has seen both famine and fortune.

Having homeschooled her two children from kindergarten through high school, Denise wasn't sure if colleges would have confidence in her 'mommy transcript' or how her teens would pay for college. In the end, both attended 4-year universities on $100,000 in scholarships and both came out with cash.

Denise now coaches parents of college-bound teens, helping them achieve scholarships and admissions opportunities for their own children. Denise is the founder of Cracking the Code to FREE College.

To learn more about Denise, visit:
www.GetAheadOfTheClass.com

What's On Your Shirt?
Erin Strayer

Erin knows that triage and trauma don't just happen in the ER, they happen in the entrepreneurial world, too.

Erin's unique background in business, health, and hospitals makes her a triple threat in triaging the entrepreneurial world. Erin started young. She co-owned a multi-million-dollar company by the age of 26 and launched a career spanning over 24 years in Level I Trauma Cardiac Surgery. Training teams on efficiency, productivity, team building, communication, and procedures in these high stress environments, Erin realized that the key was always centered around the ability to shift perspectives and that there's always another way to do the same thing – right.

Now Erin works with female entrepreneurs who are ready to scale beyond their current growth mindset, who are looking for more than a band-aid solution to their businesses' cash hemorrhages. Entrepreneurs hire Erin to provide executive level scaling strategies and accountability. Her clients create easily implementable growth strategies and get it done attitudes.

To learn more about Erin, visit:
www.erinstrayer.com
Or listen to her podcast at:
https://www.erinstrayer.com/the-erin-strayer-show

The Skeen Machine
Ilene Skeen

 **Ilene** is a speaker, author, and mentor specializing in work/life relationships for teens and adults. Her online mentoring service is available worldwide through Zoom (free software).

Ilene has had a passion for practical thinking since childhood. Her favorite pastimes were coloring books and jigsaw puzzles. These pastimes gave her thinking both a creative and analytical focus.

She is a retired business systems designer and executive. Ilene has a BS in Education, an MBA in Operations Research and Management, and a Masters in Anthropology. She is the author of ***Liftoff: The Self-Empowerment Guide for Teens***.

https://amazon.com/dp/B01H3YJ5VK

To learn more about Ilene, send her an email:
Ilene.skeen@gmail.com,
Subject: Make It A Great Day.

Let Time Do Its Job
Iman Aghay

Iman is a serial entrepreneur, international best-selling author, and world-class speaker. His TEDx talk: "Nothing to Regret," has had over 400,000 views.

Iman arrived in Vancouver, British Columbia in 2009 with limited knowledge of English, no network, and no job. To help him build his English and his confidence, Iman founded The Entrepreneurs International Network, a group of business networks that are now in five countries with over 120,000 members. After studying some of the most successful businesses in the world, Iman created a marketing system that combines the most effective online and in-person strategies.

In 2010, Iman launched Success Road Academy, which is now one of the largest information marketing training centers in the world. In just a few short years, Iman has helped thousands of people build successful businesses.

To learn more about Iman, visit:
www.SuccessRoadAcademy.com

Don't Hold Back
Jeannette Bridoux

Jeannette is a speaker, writer, and podcaster.

After overcoming depression in her teens and as a young adult, Jeannette started her podcast, Broken to Breakthrough.

Jeannette wants to give others hope for their future no matter what challenges they're facing; she interviews incredible people who have experienced life-changing circumstances and challenges. Jeannette's currently writing a book about the journey through depression and spiritual transformation that changed her life.

To learn more about Jeannette, visit:
https://www.linkedin.com/in/jeannettebridoux/

And Then There Were Elephants
and Leaving Shouldville
Jackie Simmons

Jackie is an award-winning entrepreneur, best-selling author, and TEDx speaker. Jackie's best known for creating inventive ways to simplify complex concepts and make them fun and easy to remember. Raising a daughter with suicidal thoughts taught Jackie that every day is precious and that it's not always possible to understand what someone else is going through. It is, however, completely possible to love them anyway. Jackie believes that if you know someone who's been "down" just a bit too long, don't wait – hug them now and join the movement to make suicide a thing of the past.

Learn more at:
www.TeenSuicidePreventionSociety.com

To learn more about Jackie, visit:
www.JackieSimmons.com

Ten Words of Wisdom I Wish I Had as A Teen
Jessica Peterson

Jessica is a TEDx speaker, certified business and life coach, and bestselling author of six books, including, *Create the Perfect Day.*

After a 20-year career and top sales in the banking, mortgage, and financial world, Jessica stepped into her dream and created a company to provide a positive impact for the businesses she served and their clients. Jessica is a licensed real estate agent and founder of Simply WOW Agency.

She is creating a community of WOW Power Players who are all on a mission to WOW their clients, increase their income, and create a WOW life for themselves! She used her simple plan to grow an affiliate team of over 3, 000 sales associates worldwide in one year and was selected as top speaker and trainer out of 260,000 people. Her business partner in real estate is the amazing Kevin Cottrell, who closed 240 loans in one year working limited evenings and weekends. Are you ready to WOW people, increase your business, and create a WOW life yourself? Don't miss out on your WOW!

To learn more about Jessica, visit:
www.simplywowagency.com and www.luxourteam.com

Start As Soon as You Wake Up
Joyce Blue

 **Joyce** is a certified transformational business, mindset, life and Rapid Results coach who helps women break free of self-esteem issues and take consistent action to become financially fit, emotionally secure, and more confident so they can live the lives they love, even if they have been struggling for years.

She is passionate about empowering women entrepreneurs to master their relationship with money so all of their relationships can thrive.

Joyce has studied under world-renowned mindset expert John Assaraf since 2015. She is an international Amazon #1 best-selling author.

She has been featured on Let's Do Influencing, Triumph & Tiaras, and Business Blast podcasts as well as Real, Raw & Relevant TV. Joyce has also been featured in Focus on Fabulous Magazine, OppLoans, Fit Small Business, Newsday, Thrive Global, and more.

To learn more about Joyce, visit: Life Enhancement Coaching L.L.C. on Facebook & Instagram @empoweringyoulec or email: Info@empoweringyoulec.com

No More Programs
Joy Resor

Joy inspires love, peace, and joy through her presence and offerings. She loves writing books that inspire readers and serving clients as their spiritual mentor.

To learn more about Joy, visit: joyonyourshoulders.com

Manual For Misfits
Kate Frank

Kate has always been a champion for misfits.

Her personal blog, PassionForImperfection.com, expresses her belief in those who don't easily blend into the crowd.

However, she makes a living as a professional book coach and ghostwriter at AuthorityRedefined.com. She developed a process for thought leaders to tell their stories and share their concepts as a book author. Her unique approach is to focus on the book author becoming profitable.

To learn more about Kate, reach out to her by email: Kate@AuthorityRedefined.com

Make A Stranger Smile, Today
and How To Do an Impossible Task
Ken Streater

Ken is a social-good entrepreneur, adventure travel outfitter, speaker and author.

As a founder of various businesses, consultant to Fortune 500 clients, and international river guide, Ken has traveled, worked, and played in over 50 countries. His writings are based on eye-opening experiences in places such as isolated Siberian River villages never before visited by Westerners, Botswanan delta waters plied by angry hippos, hardscrabble Alaskan subsistence villages, and a stunned Hong Kong during the Tiananmen Square uprising.

Ken runs companies, writes, and speaks in order to foster supportive and flourishing cultures. His books offer insights into everyday heroes who create meaningful individual and community change. He shares ideas for our greater good, concepts born of interactions with wise elders and young visionaries around the world. Ken believes that we each have the ability and obligation to outsize our positive impact in local communities and across the globe. He presents striking reasons why now is the time to do this.

To learn more about Ken, visit:
www.KenStreater.com or www.gudvyb.com

To Stay or To Go
Katie Miller

Katie resides in Maryland with her husband, teenage son, two parakeets, and one pet mouse.

Katie is a virtual event producer, course creation mentor, and owner of Online Course Solutions. Katie is also co-founder of the Teen Suicide Prevention Society, along with her mother and sisters. Supporting the Teen Suicide Prevention Society and The Suicide Prevention Show, Katie Miller learned she had a knack for tech.

Katie started her own business helping other speakers/mentors/coaches get their messages out into the world. Whether unraveling tech tangles or running the tech for a summit, Katie reduces your stress with her calming presence and lets you focus on what you do best . . . sharing your message to make the world a better place.

To learn more about Katie, visit:
www.sociatap.com/KT4Tech

Become The Person You Want to Be
Lil Barcaski

Lil does ghostwriting, copy editing, content (developmental editing) coaching, and publishing. On a personal note, Lil wants to be a Pulitzer Prize-winning playwright! Lil loves theater, writing plays and scripts, and playing "script doctor" for other playwrights.

Lil plays drums in a blues band and is an eclectic artist at heart, who also boogie board surfs and loves the ocean. Lil says: "Surfing is my religion. It's all about knowing how to deal with the waves, which ones to go over, which ones to go through, and which ones to surf!"

To learn more about Lil, visit:
www.VirtualCreatives.com

U B U
Kris Bell

Kris: "I was born and raised in Helena, Montana. I would say I had a pretty good childhood; I would much rather play and visit with others instead of concentrating on school stuff. But I did ok. I hung in there until graduation. After that, I didn't really know what I wanted to do when I 'grew up.'

I am very creative; and with my love for art, I decided to go to graphic arts school in Billings, Montana. I started my family early and was blessed to be a stay-at-home mom until my two girls reached school age. Then I pursued a real estate career. I loved working with people, but I still was missing something: something my soul was meant to do here on this Earth. As I matured and started looking for the 'meaning of life,' I was able to get in touch with my artsy self. I found this brought me great pleasure and inner peace.

To this day, I work in many different mediums ... stained glass, photography, painting, feather art, taxidermy ... just doing what makes me happy and peaceful. It has taken me many years to follow my heart and desires, and embrace my weirdness, and let go of what others think is good for me. My advice: find your inner joy, inner peace, make time for you to do this for you. Embrace yourself! Life is just better that way. Shine your truest form of you, the world will be a better place."

Move The Wall
Linnea Appleby

Linnea owns and operates Lime Tree Management which provides third-party management, and consulting to the self-storage industry. After growing up in New Jersey, she has been a resident of Sarasota, Florida, for 30 years.

She has a Finance degree from University of South Florida and is married to her high school sweetheart. They have two dogs and two cats. Linnea is very involved in animal rescue and operates a fundraiser for animal and other good causes called Jewelry to the Rescue. Her other interests are sewing, reading, jewelry making, and racquetball.

Those Darker Years
Mary Schrank

Mary is a former corporate healthcare executive and chronic yo-yo dieter turned health and fitness coach, and entrepreneur, helping people build home businesses and stay "ON THE WAGON" of healthy living.

Mary spent over 23 years as a healthcare executive, most of those years taking care of our greatest generation as a nursing home administrator.

In 2012, she began her entrepreneurial journey as CEO and Founder of Team Faithfully Fit LLC. Not only helping customers to stop the crazy yo-yo dieting madness by creating consistency in healthy habits that are sustainable, but also helping other entrepreneurs to build their own coaching businesses as well.

Mary enjoys her free time with husband Paul and adult son Jake, and their two fur babies Max and Maggie. "Getting you healthy 'between the ears' is a critical first step. Establishing a healthy, positive mindset will set you up for success in all aspects of your life. We'll never get your body to respond until your mind is on board."

Mary believes strongly that it is God's divine PURPOSE for her life to serve His Kingdom by coaching His children to consistently operate from their place of greatness!

Night Sky and Brain Food
Nadine Vernon

Nadine is a former educator and education administrator who worked in the field for 30+ years. She remains passionate about education.

Information is empowering. Building relationships that enable people to experience appreciation and personal satisfaction are key components of growth, whether in business or life in general.

Her creative and no nonsense let's-figure-this-out attitude enables her to help others. Remember to always reach out with kindness and put your best face forward.

To learn more about Nadine, visit:
www.NadineVernon.com

I Shouldn't Be Here
Stephanie Ashton

Stephanie lives a fulfilling and joyful life in Sarasota, Florida, with her husband and their two dogs. Stephanie regularly speaks to groups about not quitting on yourself.

She's been a mental health warrior her whole life and a chronic illness warrior for 22 years. Her friends lovingly nicknamed her "Sassy" for her perspective on life.

To learn more about Stephanie, follow her on Facebook: https://www.facebook.com/stephanie.j.hull

What Makes It a Great Day?
Mike Jones

Mike: "Who am I to have an idea for a book like this? Ever since I was a kid, I've liked helping others. I recall being in the church youth group in the 6th grade and always asking if I could help in some way, even if was setting chairs or getting ready for whatever activity we were going to do. It was not long after I realized our main purpose on this 3rd rock from the sun is to be in service of others. Think about it . . . any occupation you can think of from attorney to mechanic to zookeeper, they are all serving others in some way.

It's a nice thought and really is part of my core beliefs, although it didn't help me with my direction in life as far as my own profession goes. There were a few who made suggestions but for me a simple suggestion wasn't enough, and I often found myself discouraged.

Hence the idea for this book, if my writing, or anyone else's writing within these pages helps You to not be discouraged, then this book is a success. There are ten little words that someone put in just the right order to make BIG sense, here they are for you:

'IF IT IS TO BE, IT IS UP TO ME'

I know that kinda sounds funny. The truth: even a book like this, took a great team and countless hours to put together.

We all want support from friends and family, but it starts with the person in the mirror. Remember, you can always find someone to talk to. Each day is a gift of 86,400 seconds - take advantage of each one and "Make It A Great Day!"

Even With Dog Turds!
Valerie I. LaBoy

Valerie is a central New Jersey native who now makes her home in Southwest Florida. She is a Realtor® specializing in helping people find the right home in their newly selected state.

To learn more about Valerie, visit: www.FindMyLanai.com

Lust For Life
Rebeca Forero

Rebeca is the operations manager, Spanish interpreter, and staff leader at The Intraespa Intercultural Learning Center. She's also the co-owner of Blue Tie Events and certified in coaching and Pounding (note: Pounding is a fitness dance with drumsticks).

To learn more about Rebeca, visit:
www.BlueTieEvents.com

Hairy Legs
Shauna E. VanderHoek

Shauna is the author of *Taming Time - the small business owners guide to more time, money, and fun* and known as the "Business Whisperer."

Her background is in large-scale project management and her gift is bringing those skills to small businesses.

Animals As Teachers and Healers!
Wendy Cooper MSW

Wendy enjoyed a thriving psychotherapy practice. Later, she felt a strong call to animal communication ("AC"). Now, her AC clients get relief from grief over a sick or deceased pet, clarity about their readiness to transition, data about the pet's preferences, and fun . . . all from the pet's perspective.

All sessions are by phone. Wendy uses many forms of energetic healing.

She teaches international classes via the phone. Students learn how to do AC with their pets, even if only to let the pets know when they will return home after an absence, and how to say, "I love you," telepathically. Wendy is co-author of the renowned book, "The Spirit of Women Entrepreneurs." Wendy's mission is to be a voice for the animals, to assist humans to be in harmony with all species, and to guide people to live as their best selves with and for their pets.

To learn more about Wendy, visit:
www.AnimalCommunication.biz

And remember,
no matter what's happening around you . . .

Make It A Great Day

The Choice Is Yours!

Enjoy reading this book?

We invite you to leave a review
on Amazon and Goodreads

Made in the USA
Middletown, DE
09 October 2022

12243138R00102